You Can Have an Amazing Life... in just 60 days!

Also by Dr. John F. Demartini

*How to Make One Hell of a Profit and Still Get to Heaven

*The Breakthrough Experience:
A Revolutionary New Approach to Personal Transformation

Count Your Blessings: The Healing Power of Gratitude and Love

*Available from Hay House

✦✦✦✦✦

Hay House Titles of Related Interest

Attitude Is Everything for Success: Say It, Believe It, Receive It,
by Keith D. Harrell

Empowerment: You Can Do, Be, and Have All Things,
by John Randolph Price

Life Is Short—Wear Your Party Pants: Ten Simple Truths That
Lead to an Amazing Life, by Loretta LaRoche

10 Secrets for Success and Inner Peace, by Dr. Wayne W. Dyer

You Can Heal Your Life, by Louise L. Hay

✦✦✦✦✦

All of the above are available at your local bookstore,
or may be ordered by visiting:

Hay House USA: **www.hayhouse.com**
Hay House Australia: **www.hayhouse.com.au**
Hay House UK: **www.hayhouse.co.uk**
Hay House South Africa: **orders@psdprom.co.za**
Hay House India: **www.hayhouseindia.co.in**

You Can Have an Amazing Life... in just 60 days!

Dr. John F. Demartini

HAY
HOUSE

HAY HOUSE, INC.
Carlsbad, California
London • Sydney • Johannesburg
Vancouver • Hong Kong • New Delhi

Copyright © 2005 by John F. Demartini

Published and distributed in the United States by: Hay House, Inc.: www.hayhouse.com • **Published and distributed in Australia by:** Hay House Australia Pty. Ltd.: www.hayhouse.com.au • **Published and distributed in the United Kingdom by:** Hay House UK, Ltd.: www.hayhouse.co.uk • **Published and distributed in the Republic of South Africa by:** Hay House SA (Pty), Ltd.: orders@psdprom.co.za • **Distributed in Canada by:** Raincoast: www.raincoast.com • **Published in India by:** Hay House Publishers India: www.hayhouseindia.co.in

Editorial supervision: Jill Kramer • *Design:* Jenny Richards

Library of Congress Cataloging-in-Publication Data

Demartini, John F.
You can have an amazing life—in just 60 days! / John F. Demartini.
p. cm.
      ISBN 1-4019-0550-1 (tradepaper)
1. Self-actualization (Psychology) I. Title.

BF637.S4D46 2005
158.1—dc22
                           2004018565

ISBN 13: 978-1-4019-0550-7
ISBN 10: 1-4019-0550-1

09 08 07 06   5 4 3 2
1st printing, February 2005
2nd printing, November 2006

Printed in the United States of America

This special book is for those individuals who would truly love to live a free and amazing life, for those who feel inspired or called from within to be someone extraordinary, or do and have something astonishing.

We all have the potential for greatness and the capacity to leave a legacy, but so often we dishonor our true and radiant selves and those we love by not giving ourselves permission to shine and let our amazing selves out.

My dream is to have this special book act as a catalyst for such a release and transformation. May you now live such an amazing life, and may the next 60 days change you forever.

Contents

Introduction

Right now you're probably in a bookstore, coffee shop, library, or conference room—or perhaps you're in a comfortable chair or bed at home—while previewing this unique and life-changing book. As familiar as your surroundings may be, you're about to experience an incredible shift and awaken to a brand-new you. Get ready to embark on a journey that could not only transform you, but also prompt others to exclaim, "Wow, you truly live an amazing life!"

How do I know that this journey awaits you? As I've traveled the world, I've heard the above comment from all kinds of people. And if I'm blessed to receive such words simply by living the laws I present in this special book, then there's no reason why you can't experience exactly the same thing.

Within these pages, I'll reveal 60 inspiring laws that *anyone* can follow. They're the very ones that have enabled me to live a truly fulfilling life. You see, since the age of 17, I've dedicated myself to studying and sharing universal truths, especially as they apply to personal growth and healing. This has taken me from living as a surf bum and high school dropout to the life of my dreams—with abundant wealth in all areas: spiritual, mental, professional, financial, familial, social, and physical.

What you're about to read is the result of more than three decades of research and 20-plus years of clinical experience as a chiropractor, healer, and teacher. My road to these professions has hardly been traditional, and it's certainly been bumpy. Born with several physical deformities, I was later told that I'd never read or write very well. By then, I'd overcome my body's limitations and fallen in love with sports, and I dreamed of being a world-class surfer.

As an adolescent, I was moved to a new school when my family relocated from Houston to Richmond, Texas. Although I'd gained a reputation among my old classmates for being an athlete, at this new place I became known as a punching bag for the local bullies. Disheartened by my academic prospects and frightened by the violence at school, I sought the support of my parents to let me go to California to surf. At 14, I hitchhiked west and stayed in beach towns up and down the coast, living hand to mouth and meeting other surfers who helped me get by.

I rode some of the biggest waves in California before moving on to an island paradise on the north shore of Oahu, Hawaii, where I surfed from sunrise to sunset, lived in a tent, and ate whatever hung low on the tropical trees. It was very "back to nature," and I was quite content, but there was one problem: Unknowingly, I consumed a poison in the form of the toxic seeds of the woodrose plant. In time, the strychnine accumulated in my system and caused me to become seriously ill. After I'd spent nearly four days unconscious in my tent, a woman from the jungle happened by and helped me walk to the local health-food store. I was 17.

Slowly, I began to recover. But one thing weighed on my mind: At the health-food store, I'd seen a poster for Dr. Paul C. Bragg, a naturopath, longevitist, physical therapist, and health consultant to movie stars, as well as Jack La Lanne's teacher. I became determined to see Dr. Bragg speak when he came to Hawaii just a couple weeks after my ordeal.

When the day arrived, I hitchhiked to the presentation. With great power and precision, then-93-year-old Dr. Bragg delivered a truly profound message. I was transfixed by how wise and physically vibrant he was—at one point, he even leaned over into a handstand and continued his presentation upside down without missing a beat. Near the end of his talk, he announced that it was time for everyone to determine their purpose and vision. What special mission would we dedicate the rest of our lives to?

I was stunned. How was I supposed to know this? But Dr. Bragg helped by guiding us in something he called *the Alpha Meditation.* During this experience, I cemented my desires: I wanted to research the laws of the universe as they related to the body, mind, and soul, particularly as they could lead me to healing and traveling. I'd share my findings with people and get paid for it. At the end of the meditation, I was teary-eyed, inspired, and on fire: I would be a teacher, healer, and philosopher.

Big dreams, right? They seemed especially grandiose for a high school dropout/surfer who'd just walked away from death's door and was still living in a tent, not to mention having some serious learning disabilities. So I approached Dr. Bragg later and shared my predicament. He told me that I could overcome all this if I just did one thing (which *you'll* discover on Day 6 of this book).

His advice certainly bore fruit. At 18, I returned home to Texas, took and passed my high school equivalency exam, then attended college in pursuit of my dream of becoming a healer.

Years later, it humbles me to reflect on my journey from the difficult classrooms of my youth, to the beaches of Oahu, to the crisp clinical office I ran for years, to the stages all over the world where I now deliver a message that still stirs my soul. What moved me then, and what keeps going me today, are the laws you'll be reading about and applying in this book.

You can have the life of your dreams, too, simply by being the already amazing individual you are right now! Yes, you have what it takes to transform wherever you are to the place you'd love to be.

Just imagine for a moment . . . you're living a magnificent, fruitful, wonderful life! Envisioning this is the first step. If you then read the laws of life in this book and let them sink in, allowing yourself to gradually incorporate their essence into your daily actions, their wisdom will awaken your spirit to the wonderful power within, and you'll shine. Your magnificence is about to surface and become even more evident in the actions, presence, and outcomes of your new life.

It inspires me to think about the difference you could make for yourself—as well as for others—simply by applying these laws on a daily basis, and it excites me to think what could happen to you in just two short months if you began concentrating on a single law each day.

Among the thousands of people I've been privileged to counsel and help guide to the center of their being, I've found that every one of them is filled with tremendous power. Let's now work together and begin to awaken your amazing life.

How to Use This Book

Although this guide is designed to take you through a powerful, 60-day process for creating your new life, it would be wise to read it once—straight through from cover to cover—then sit down and contemplate what you've just encountered. Give yourself a day's breather and then begin again, rereading each of the laws in order, one per day for the next 60 days. You'll notice that each new principle contributes to the others—that is, they're interdependent and overlap, which increases their power in your life, adding strength with each variation. Don't feel that you must memorize this process, since it's all been constructed with the idea of constant reinforcement and building on what you've already integrated.

At the close of each law of life, you'll see a section called "Words of Power." These are meant as meaningful and inspiring statements that you can say to yourself, inwardly or outwardly, and hold as true from the center of your being. They're powerful statements that you'll know at a deep level are speaking about your destiny, and which will assist you in embodying the laws to the fullest.

Rather than lopsided affirmations or negations, these are balanced and inspiring statements by which you can live a fulfilling life—simple truths calling you to live more profoundly in their presence—so be ready to watch your life change and your dreams become more realized as time goes by.

At the end of each day's reading, repeat that law's Words of Power seven times, and then use them as examples and ideas to create personalized statements—known as "My Words of Power." (There's space for you to write them down near the end of each chapter.) Use words and phrases you'd love to say to yourself every day, and make sure that they're in the present tense: *I am, I do, I see, I live—now!* Try pulling some powerful, truthful words from each of the laws of life, and as they resonate within you, they'll transform your day and help you enjoy a more amazing journey . . . the life of your dreams.

Finally, sit silently and reflect on the law of the day and note any intuitive insights that arise in the closing section of each chapter, "My Reflections." This will also help you incorporate the law and its wise actions into your daily life.

Let's review this process from the beginning: After you've read the entire book straight through in order to just let the laws wash over you, please begin it again so that you can integrate the individual principles more deeply. Then, each day for 60 days:

- **Read one law.** (Be sure to read them in order; don't skip around.)

- **Read the law's Words of Power** and repeat them seven times.

- **Create "My Words of Power"** using your own language and any phrases that inspire you from that day, then repeat them seven times.

- **Take a few moments to reflect** on the day's reading and record any insights that come to you.

A FEW MORE WORDS ABOUT YOUR REFLECTIONS

You can begin using the laws today to fulfill your life's purpose, dreams, and objectives by simply putting yourself in a state of gratitude and writing whatever your heart and soul whisper to you. Think about everything you're thankful for, which makes you inspired, gives you fulfillment, and brings tears to your eyes. Then quiet your mind, see what comes to you, and record it in the space provided ("My Reflections"). As you write, you'll discover more about who you are and what you'd truly love to become, do, and have. By acting upon such inspired messages, you can begin to live the fulfilling life of your dreams.

This time will often be transformational because it clarifies and crystallizes your desires and awakens purposefulness. During the 60 days that you spend with this book, you'll receive messages and visions, and you'll find yourself thinking of ways to fulfill your destiny. Write them on the lines provided in this book, reflect on your inner wisdom, and review these pages often, refining them as needed while you watch your visions unfold.

Your Words of Power, reflections, insights, dreams, and visions will come alive through this practice because the power of manifestation begins in writing about what truly inspires you. Bring your mind down from your head into your heart, and begin from that place. This is your book, written for you, so make it your own.

You're amazing! You're here to live your life magnificently, and this book will show you how to dream effectively—and how to live the life you dream. So let's get started.

Week
ONE

Day 1
The Law of Love

When I was in the first grade, a teacher told me that I'd probably never be able to read, write, or communicate very well because of my learning difficulties and dyslexia. It seemed as though she might be right as I struggled through a few more grades then dropped out of school in my early teens. But after my near-death experience at age 17 and interaction with an elderly mentor who turned my life around, I found myself miraculously passing and earning my general equivalency diploma (GED).

With this new and unexpected success behind me, I began to dream about what I might become. At that time, I was living with my parents in Richmond, Texas, and I imagined that I'd somehow overcome my limitations to become a great teacher, healer, and philosopher who'd travel the world and share my research findings. Earning a degree was an important first step, and with my parents' help, I was able to attend a local junior college.

After my first test in American history, I received notification that I'd significantly failed. A score of 72 was necessary to pass, but I'd scored 27. I was so distraught that while driving home I was brought to tears. When I reached my parents' house, I curled up into a little ball in their living room and continued to weep. I thought that my life's dream was shattered.

As if by some higher design, my mother walked in a few moments later and saw me there on the floor. She asked, "Son, what's wrong? What's happened?"

I sobbed, "Mom, I just bombed my history test! I required a 72 to pass, and I received a 27. I guess I'm still dyslexic—even my test scores are in reverse. It looks like my first-grade teacher was right: I'll never be able to read, write, or even communicate."

My mother looked me right in the eye and with great love, said, "Son, whether you become a great teacher, healer, and philosopher, or go back to your life as a great surfer, I just want to let you know that your father and I are going to love you, no matter what."

When she said that, my distress and despair disappeared. I remember putting my hand into a fist, looking up into the air, and *seeing* my dream of being a great teacher, healer, and philosopher. I wanted to travel the world, and as I saw it so clearly, I said to myself, *I'll do whatever it takes! I'll travel whatever distance, and pay whatever price, just so that I can teach and give my services of love!*

Because my mother cared enough to open her heart and make that loving statement, she introduced me to a true and empowering state of unconditional love. In that moment, I again caught a glimpse of the gift of my own magnificence. She helped me transform a truly desolate moment into one of concrete commitment, and because of that, I've gotten where I am today.

You probably influence people, too, such as your children, family members, or co-workers. Know that if you love them for who they are, your heart will gleam, shine, and reach out to share that love, and you'll make a difference in their lives. They'll become more, accomplish more, and have more in their lives—and so will you. The power of unconditional love is unsurpassed in its power to transform.

Everyone longs to be cherished for who they are, and if you share the truth of your heart just as my mother so graciously did, the people in your circle will become the wondrous individuals they're capable of being.

The Law of Love is the supreme law, the one that all the others support you in moving toward and honoring. As you'll see, all the following chapters will lead you back here. Hold the Law of Love close, and feel your heart reach out, spreading your amazing life further than you may have thought possible.

WORDS OF POWER

No matter what I have done or not done, I am worthy of love.
Love is all there is. All else is illusion.
My life is a life of love.
I love others no matter what they have done or not done.
I am surrounded by love 24 hours day.
I am thankful for all the love that is.
Love is the greatest of all healers.

MY WORDS OF POWER

_____

_____

_____

_____

_____

_____

_____

_____

MY REFLECTIONS

How can I use the Law of Love today to fulfill my life's
purpose, dreams, and objectives?

_____

_____

_____

_____

_____

_____

_____

_____

✦ ✦ ✦ ✦ ✦

Day 2
The Law of Inspiration

As I travel the world and speak in front of audiences, one of the most frequent comments I receive from the lovely people in attendance is, "That was so inspiring!"

When someone tells me this, *I'm* inspired, enthusiastic about what's in store for him or her, and energized to keep working toward my own hopes and dreams. Encouraging others to pursue and achieve what they'd truly love is one of the most personally empowering things I can do: When I move others to do what they long for, they'll help me do the same—it's the ultimate win-win.

How can *you* generate and communicate such inspiration and maintain an inspired state yourself?

I've been seeking these answers for many years and have discovered that there's actually a science to it: the regular application of gratitude. If you're ungrateful in light of events that have occurred because you perceive them as "bad," you live in fear with guilt and desperation. But when you're thankful for whatever happens, regardless of how you might perceive it in the moment, you live in love with inspiration, for when you're truly appreciative—no matter the circumstance—life becomes more meaningful and fulfilling.

Following are a couple of secret action steps (not so secret anymore!) for living in an attitude of gratitude. Do these each day, and they'll help you be more thankful:

1. Every single morning before you rise and shine, and every
    night before you fall asleep, spend 5 to 15 minutes thinking
    about all the experiences for which you can say thank you and
    write them down. I keep a notepad and pen on the night table
    so that I can do this, and it often fills me with an inspiration so
    intense that I sometimes find myself in tears.

2. After you've eaten lunch, simply take a few deep breaths, sit
    and meditate for a moment, and enter into a state of gratitude.
    Think about what you can appreciate and then ask yourself
    (that is, your inner source, mind, or soul): *Do you have some-
    thing for me today?*

When I do this, an inspiring message or vision will enter my mind,
letting me know what wise action to take or what's next in my life, and
I write that down. When I get another revelation, I write that one down,
too. I fill my life with these stirring ideas.

To paraphrase Henry David Thoreau, most people live quiet lives of
desperation, not invigorating lives of inspiration—not doing what they
love nor loving what they do. They aren't grateful, so they're stepping
on the brakes rather than pushing the accelerator. They're blaming circumstances and the world around them instead of being inspired and
fueled by them.

When the dazzling messages on the inside become greater than
everyone else's opinions on the outside, you've mastered your life and
are living by inspiration, not desperation.

Become a person of greater understanding and wisdom: Follow your
heart and *let* yourself be grateful! Each day, think about what you've
gained, given, learned, taught, or experienced that's valuable to you.
Before going to bed and before you rise, focus on what you can appreciate, and then ask for guidance from your innermost being. Watch the
ideas come to you, and then act on them. When you follow your impulse
of thanksgiving, you won't be distracted from what's truly important,
and you'll build your dreams.

Often people say, "Oh, how I wish I'd followed my intuition on . . ."

Don't do this to yourself! Instead, train yourself daily to listen to and follow your inner voice. If you back this up with gratitude every single day, you'll live a brilliant life. Follow the Amazing Law of Inspiration. Make it your life, and honor your magnificence.

WORDS OF POWER

Every day and every night, I count my blessings.
I am inspired. I am enthused. I am powerful.
I am grateful for all that is, as it is, and it inspires me.
I follow my intuition and inspiration and am
thankful for all my blessings.
The inspired vision of my innermost being
is greater than all the opinions I hear from without.
I am an inspired being with an inspired vision and message.

MY WORDS OF POWER

_____

_____

_____

_____

_____

_____

_____

MY REFLECTIONS

How can I use the Law of Inspiration today to fulfill my life's
purpose, dreams, and objectives?

_____

_____

_____

_____

_____

_____

_____

◆◆◆◆◆

Day 3
The Law of Quality Questions

Notice the difference between the following:

1. "I'd love to travel and go overseas, perhaps to Asia, but how could I ever pay for that?"

2. "I'd love to go to Asia. How can I go there and get paid for it?"

Each option clearly leads to a different outcome because your life moves in relation to the quality of your questions. Likewise, if you ask, "How am I ever going to pay my bills? How am I going to afford that?" you'll limit yourself to your stated outcomes: paying bills and affording things. But if you inquire, "How do I get paid to do exactly what I love?" you'll get something else entirely: financial rewards for enjoying yourself.

This chapter provides you with great questions to use in your life. Because I've asked these of myself for many years, I know that they'll be useful to you, and I recommend working with them again and again.

1. Begin with this: **"What would I absolutely love to do in my life?"** At first you might think, *I don't know.* But give yourself a minute, and the ideas will come. Then just start listing everything you love, even if it seems insignificant. Keep adding and refining all that you'd love to be, do, and have in your life.

2. Next, write: **"How do I get handsomely, beautifully, and incredibly paid to do this?"** Although this may stump you initially, simply keep asking, and suddenly creative concepts will begin to flow as to how you can earn magnificently by following your passion. Write down all your thoughts, even if they seem impossible or crazy or far-fetched. Keep adding details and even more ideas.

3. **"What are the seven highest priority action steps that I can do today to make that happen?"** After you've written all seven, put them in the order of their priority to you.

4. Then answer this: **"What obstacles might I encounter, and how can I solve them in advance?"** When you respond, you'll have your contingencies in place.

5. After covering these basics, ask, **"How can I do it more effectively and efficiently?"** Think! The solutions here can substantially alter your productivity and fulfillment.

6. Don't forget to look backward as well as forward: **"What worked today, and what didn't?"** Listen to the feedback from your inner source and hone in on even more quality actions and questions you can follow up on.

7. The final query that I've found extremely powerful in helping me get what I'd love in life is, **"How did whatever happened—whether positive or negative—serve me?"** See the benefits, and learn lessons from whatever has happened in your life.

Remember, when you ask quality questions, your life changes. Let's recap so that you have a handy reference for all seven questions.

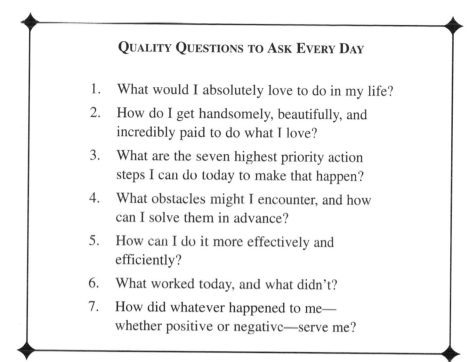

QUALITY QUESTIONS TO ASK EVERY DAY

1. What would I absolutely love to do in my life?

2. How do I get handsomely, beautifully, and incredibly paid to do what I love?

3. What are the seven highest priority action steps I can do today to make that happen?

4. What obstacles might I encounter, and how can I solve them in advance?

5. How can I do it more effectively and efficiently?

6. What worked today, and what didn't?

7. How did whatever happened to me— whether positive or negative—serve me?

I guarantee that if you ask these seven questions of yourself every single day, without fail, and if you truly look for and pay attention to the answers, you'll be more fulfilled and inspired.

Make your life the amazing one you deserve to live by employing the Law of Quality Questions. It can change your life forever, and you'll make a difference if you start today.

WORDS OF POWER

I ask myself quality questions every day. I live a quality life.
I define and pursue the life of my dreams.
I live the life I love.

MY WORDS OF POWER

_____
_____
_____
_____
_____
_____
_____
_____

MY REFLECTIONS

How can I use the Law of Quality Questions today to fulfill
my life's purpose, dreams, and objectives?

_____
_____
_____
_____
_____
_____
_____

✦✦✦✦✦

Day 4
The Law of Blessings

A number of years ago when I was visiting my dad, he asked, "Son, how are things going?"

I replied, "Well, I've expanded my office, so I had to pay the build-out costs and taxes, and right now I'm short of capital. I bought diamond rings for my wife and me, plus the new car, and we just went on a vacation to Hawaii and got a new house.

"A whole bunch of things are going on, and it seems as if it's all happening at once. With all this spending, we don't have as much cash as usual, I'm totally overwhelmed, my gums are bleeding, and my eyes are itchy—every part of me is stressed."

He looked at me and chuckled, "Son, that's not stress. That's blessings!"

"What do you mean?" I answered.

He explained, "John, what you've accomplished in a short period of time is more than I've done in 30 years. Your mother and I have never gone to Hawaii. We still haven't got diamond rings—we just have simple gold bands. You've got more diamonds than we do. And by the way, the idea of expanding your office is incredible. The extra taxes and things—just consider that a blessing because it means you've earned some money."

He took every single thing I thought was a "stressing," and he made them all blessings. I ended up with tears in my eyes because of his wisdom: I saw it one way, but he helped me to view everything in an entirely different light.

I grew up hearing my mother talk about this law, but I'd gotten so caught up in my daily affairs that I'd forgotten it. From the time I was nearly four years old, as she was putting me to bed, she'd remind me, "Son, count your blessings tonight, for those who do will have more to be grateful for, and more opportunities in their lives, than those who don't."

This simple teaching is so powerful that I wrote about it in detail in my book *Count Your Blessings*. I can say without a doubt that if you take the time to notice and be grateful for what you have—no matter what it feels like right now—your life will certainly change.

Pause every single day to just stop and think of what you can give thanks for, and then record it in an ongoing list. I have an entire book containing only a long inventory of such wonders. Whenever I feel a little stressed, I open that volume, and it changes my perspective.

The Law of Blessings is one of the most powerful forces you'll ever have in your life. So be grateful, and count your blessings every day!

WORDS OF POWER

I count my blessings daily.
My life is a constant stream of blessings.
The more I am grateful, the more I have to be grateful for.
The more blessings I count, the more obstacles I mount.
I am blessed, and my blessings are infinite.
Everything is a gift. Thank you.

MY WORDS OF POWER

_____

_____

_____

_____

_____

_____

_____

_____

MY REFLECTIONS

How can I use the Law of Blessings today to fulfill my life's
purpose, dreams, and objectives?

_____

_____

_____

_____

_____

_____

_____

_____

Day 5
The Law of Presence

As you walk along your beautiful and challenging road of life, you may sometimes focus on past experiences or what you imagine might happen in the future. When you're entangled with guilt from yesterday's events or fear of what tomorrow may bring, you can become disempowered. These debilitating emotions result from untrue, imbalanced (exaggerated or minimized) perceptions.

When distracted by such guilt or fear, you over- or underreact to your environment and can end up exerting too much or too little time and energy—literally overdoing your daily actions or going too far the other way. Through such guilt or fear, you may also exaggerate or minimize yourself and those around you—as well as the amount of love in your environment.

At those times, it's easy to overlook the amazing and loving current moment, but when you exist in the now, you're at your most powerful and truthful; you perceive and act moderately and wisely. Since moments of fear and guilt reflect perceptual lies about your life, they can momentarily undermine your self-worth and growth until the truth of the present once again returns and sets your mind free.

Many years ago, I experienced an error-initiated IRS audit. I frantically wondered how I was going to come up with all the money the agency stated I owed. When I first received the notice, I didn't even understand exactly what the IRS was—and as an unknown, it became an even more frightening experience. But when I finally went through the auditing process, I realized it wasn't nearly as challenging as I'd imagined. I'd exaggerated things.

When I'd been frightened and in that exaggerating mode, I hadn't been *present.* My business suffered, my relationships were stressed, and everything appeared to be chaotic. Because I'd magnified the power around me and minimized the power within myself, I couldn't be in the moment. I'd been living in fear of an imagined future—and with remembered guilt—and I was definitely disempowered.

One way to recognize that the present is slipping away from you is to notice if, when you meet others, you imagine that they're better or worse than you. Realize right then that if you do this, you're either exaggerating or minimizing (which automatically generates guilt and fear) because these actions are lies you tell yourself. Fear precedes every lie, and guilt follows. Each time you deceive, exaggerate, or minimize someone or something, you disempower yourself, leave the present moment, and hide your light and truth. You get caught in remembered guilt or fear of an imaginary future.

The secret to being present is keeping a balanced *mind,* which lets your true self shine. You're enlightened when you become present: You see things not as greater or lesser, but as true and equitable. Here in this moment, the seer, seeing, and seen are all the same.

In the now, you're centered, more receptive, and more willing to listen than to speak, and you're able to attract opportunities. People who are present experience open hearts and minds because they're in a state of equilibrium. They have poise. Those who live this way lead and rule; they govern and direct.

The secret behind the Law of Presence is to look for the lovely balance. If you journey through life seeing things this way, you're able to be *there,* not lost in the past or future. Follow the Law of Presence and watch what happens to your life. See your own balanced magnificence and the beauty of the world around you.

WORDS OF POWER

I am present. I am certain. I am love.
I bring my exaggerations and my minimizations into equilibrium.

I balance my perceptions and open my heart.
I am balanced and truthful.
I am grateful for my balanced life.
I am present. I am silent, and all is in order.

MY WORDS OF POWER

_____

_____

_____

_____

_____

_____

_____

MY REFLECTIONS

How can I use the Law of Presence today to fulfill my life's
purpose, dreams, and objectives?

_____

_____

_____

_____

_____

_____

_____

Day 6
The Law of Genius

Did you know that a genius lives deep inside you? When I was 17, a wise 93-year-old man shared a personal affirmation with me. He told me to say it every single day, without fail, for the rest of my life: *I am a genius, and I apply my wisdom.*

At first, some people laughed at me when I said that out loud. I was living in Hawaii at the time, and the surfing buddies who lived with me in my tent howled hysterically. They made up my first so-called support group, so I learned to keep such inspiring words to myself until they began to manifest. More important, I realized that it doesn't matter what other people think—it's what you think about yourself that forms your life. That affirmation changed everything for me, just as my wise mentor knew it would.

I've since come to believe that *everyone* has brilliance inside. My teacher's words changed the course of my destiny, and now when I present a seminar called "Awakening Your Genius!" I watch people rouse their innermost potential with simple tools such as the ones I'm about to share with you.

First, make a list of all the individuals you consider to be geniuses in life, no matter what their chosen fields are. Whether they're in music, art, poetry, dance, science, or spirituality, write down their names, and then find and read their biographies. One time I actually made a list of all the Nobel Prize winners in every category since the award's inception. I read each Nobel Laureate's work, devouring every text I could find and scouring his or her life story.

By reading the biographies of these great people, you'll discover what I did: They're just like you and me. You have more in common with them than you may have ever imagined, and by realizing this, you'll begin to wake up a part of yourself that can more consistently inspire you.

If you put your hand into a pot of glue, some of it will stick; so, too, if you put your mind into the great works of the masters, some of their mastery will stay with you. You have brilliance inside. All that's required is associating with other geniuses by reading about their lives, and starting to apply the Law of Genius by repeating my mentor's statement of truth. This will help you begin acknowledging the inner presence of your own mastery, which is just waiting to unfold.

Tell yourself, *I am a genius, and I apply my wisdom.* Say these Words of Power to yourself every single day for the rest of your life. While stating these magic words inwardly, outward miracles begin to happen. You'll uncover your inner magnificence and begin to let yourself shine.

You see, if you say to yourself that you're a genius—if you repeat it every single day—it will start to become real for you. Two years after I began doing this, I was sitting in a library at Wharton County Junior College when a group of students began to gather around me. They asked me to tutor them in calculus, and I heard one of the young gentlemen sitting behind me whisper in awe to his friend, "That John—he's a *genius!*" At that moment, I remembered with gratitude what my 93-year-old teacher had said to me.

Simply repeat this statement to yourself every single day, and when all the parts of your body begin to believe it, so will the world. You *are* a genius. You're magnificent! Start to associate with giants, follow the Law of Genius, and watch what brilliant actions come out of your life.

WORDS OF POWER

I am a genius, and I apply my wisdom.
I am a genius who hears the messages of my soul and obeys.
I am a genius who sees the inner vision of my soul and follows.
I associate with geniuses and read their works,
and their genius sticks to me!

I am a genius, and I apply my wisdom!
I am a genius, and I apply my wisdom!
I am a genius, and I apply my wisdom!

MY WORDS OF POWER

_____

_____

_____

_____

_____

_____

_____

_____

MY REFLECTIONS

How can I use the Law of Genius today to fulfill my life's
purpose, dreams, and objectives?

_____

_____

_____

_____

_____

_____

_____

Day 7
The Law of Appreciation

Have you ever been to a dull social gathering where the host had obviously made an effort, but that bored you so thoroughly you vowed never to go to a "party" there again? And then when you got home, you thought, *Even if it wasn't so great, I still ought to write the host a thank-you note.* Feeling obligated, you sat down and wrote a blah-sounding letter, which then required editing, rewriting, and still more editing. It was a chore you just had to do, and since it wasn't something you were really inspired about, the process became tedious and draining.

What would happen if you went to another event and found it absolutely exhilarating? Perhaps you met fascinating people and learned some incredible ideas, and you thought, *Wow! What a great experience!* You talked about it all the way home and realized, *I'm inspired.* You sat down, and almost faster than you could move your pen, there flowed forth enthusiastic words of appreciation.

When you're in a state of gratitude, there's less editing, less rewriting, less redoing in your life. Likewise, an organization filled with appreciative and grateful people doesn't have as much hiring and firing, training and refining—or as much overhead—as one that isn't. You're on top of the world when you're appreciative.

This attitude has the power to integrate your body, spirit, mind, and heart. It brings out the truth of your magnificence and allows you to be present, poised, and certain. It's one of the key laws.

To appreciate life is to have fulfillment in it. Stop and think about this: When real estate prices go up, they "appreciate" in value—that is, their worth rises. The Law of Appreciation teaches you how to raise your *own* value and helps you grow. It's not only the secret of fulfillment, but it's also the secret to decreasing the need to edit or rewrite life. You have more vitality when you have appreciation than you do at any other time, so stop, reflect, and think about what you could give thanks for. Make it your aim to be appreciative of your life and acknowledge the amazing journey you experience.

The philosopher and mathematician Gottfried Wilhelm Leibniz taught me the significance of appreciation through his book *Discourse on Metaphysics,* which I first read when I was 18 years old. Now I pass the torch to you: Follow the Law of Appreciation in your life, and watch how much less self-editing you require and how amazingly refined your life becomes.

WORDS OF POWER

I appreciate my life.

My life appreciates in value as I learn to appreciate life.

My spirit and soul, my mind and heart, and my brain and body are all one when I'm appreciative.

Regardless of the pleasure or pain, I appreciate the blessings of my life.

I am fulfilled because I appreciate my life.

I take time every day to think of all that I am grateful for.

Thank you for all that is—as it is.

MY WORDS OF POWER

_____

_____

_____

_____

_____

_____

_____

_____

MY REFLECTIONS

How can I use the Law of Appreciation today to fulfill my life's
purpose, dreams, and objectives?

_____

_____

_____

_____

_____

_____

_____

_____

Week
TWO

Day 8
The Law of Vitality

Quite often people come up to me and remark, "John, I'd love to have your energy! Where do you get the enthusiasm for all you do?"

I respond, "Well, being clear on my mission and where I'm going in life has probably been my most important source of vitality." Here are seven tools that have helped me live more fully:

1. **Know where you're going.** If you have a clear road map, it's much easier to get somewhere. Your energy soars when you're clear on your aim and direction.

2. **Be thankful.** (Refer to the previous Law of Appreciation and Law of Gratitude for more information, too.) When you're thankful for your life, your power picks up, and when you're ungrateful, you shut down.

3. **Eat moderately.** Many people try to perk themselves up by pigging out, thinking that they're going to gain zest from food, but this isn't the way to do it. It's actually been shown that if you eat less, you'll have increased vitality. I don't mean that you should go on the Gandhi diet, just eat lightly or moderately. Walk away from the table feeling a little less full, rather than more so. You'll find that you have more spark to do the things you love. You might be a little thin, and that's fine—it's better to have two pounds less than that much more. Biological research shows that people live longer if they eat less, and they also have more get-up-and-go.

4. **Drink water.** Those who drink sufficient water (rather than other liquids) increase their vitality, so make sure that you stay fully hydrated every day. Even while I'm writing and speaking, I drink water, because it's the universal solvent that opens up my mind to greater understanding.

5. **Breathe fully and deeply.** My observation of some of the most magnetic and charismatic people in the world has revealed that they inhale deeply and diaphragmatically. Like Pavarotti, they breathe in with incredible *joie de vivre.*

   Why not try it now? Let your chest and abdomen fill up as you take in a deep, full breath. Continue a bit, letting the oxygen come in and the carbon dioxide go out. In Eastern philosophy and mysticism, yogis describe the breath as *prana,* or fundamental life force. Every time you inhale, you breathe in vitality, so take advantage of this.

6. **Connect your vocation and your avocation.** That is, make sure that there's a link between your work and what sets your mind and heart on fire. If you aren't doing what you love and loving what you do, you have a brake on all the time—and that's the fastest way to deplete your energy. Do you want to get run-down and distract yourself with things you don't love doing? Hardly! Define your work mission: Be clear about it and follow these principles to add vitality to life.

7. **Smile.** Smiling can change your physiology and make you look up at life, so go outside and stand in the beauty of nature. Look up into the heavens, smile, and say, "Thank you, universe! I'm grateful for the gifts I've been receiving." Your energy will pick up immediately. Not only will you have vigor in your body, but you'll also find vivacity in your mind and more vitality in your creative expressions and actions.

You'll be a more productive individual, living a more energized and amazing life, by following all seven aspects of the Law of Vitality that you've learned here.

WORDS OF POWER

I know where I am going, for I have a mission.

I take time to be grateful every day.

I eat moderately.

I drink plenty of water.

I breathe deeply as I say, "Thank you, universe!"

I smile at life and the people around me.

My vocation helps me fulfill my avocation.

I love what I do, and I do what I love.

MY WORDS OF POWER

_____

_____

_____

_____

_____

_____

_____

MY REFLECTIONS

How can I use the Law of Vitality today to fulfill my life's
purpose, dreams, and objectives?

_____

_____

_____

_____

_____

_____

_____

_____

Day 9
The Law of Silence

W hen you read the title of this chapter, perhaps you'll think that I shouldn't have to say anything about it! There would be some wisdom in that, but I *do* have a few things to tell you.

Imagine what would happen if you sat for 15 or 30 minutes (or longer) in pure silence—no distractions other than natural sounds in the environment. When you do so, your brain chatter can begin to diminish. Suddenly, clear thoughts are able to enter your mind, and solutions to unsolved problems may surface. In fact, some of the great accomplishments of human genius have been birthed in moments of silence.

This is the value of meditation, which is often misunderstood as some complicated or difficult ritual. It can be, but it can also be as simple as spending some time (however brief) in quietude to allow your mind to stop fussing over trivialities. You can do this sitting up or lying down, before or after dinner or lunch, but do find a time and place for such meditation or contemplation, a time when you simply remain in pure silence.

Every year or two, I conduct a seminar called "Four Days of Wisdom." I invite people from all over the world to come and be with me in silence. I'm often asked, "Why would someone come all the way around the globe to be quiet?" They do it because extraordinary experiences occur. Some attendees have said they've awakened a telepathic-like ability that allows them to communicate without words—that is, they started to read other people's minds. Others have claimed that they solved previously irreconcilable problems in their lives. Still others finally became clear about their mission and the direction of their lives.

When we're not talking and are truly present, we do awaken some amazing capacities. Our great minds suddenly link together, similar to a mastermind, and we start to pick up on each other's thoughts. This is powerful, because we can begin to tune in (through our intention) to almost anyone. We somehow start thinking and feeling what they are.

I encourage you to sit still, enter a state of gratitude, and contemplate for at least 15 minutes in total silence every day. Have paper and pencil ready to record any inspiring revelations or dreams that emerge.

One of my daily rituals is to enter into a state of thankfulness by counting my blessings and thinking about all the experiences or accomplishments that I truly appreciate in my life. Then I sit in silence and ask, "Universal Source of All Existence, do you have a message for me today?"

And in such moments of silence comes a whispering voice from the innermost source of my mind that answers, "Yes! Do this."

Silence is potent: It allows you to tune in to your intuition and guiding inspiration and provides solutions to problems. Give yourself this gift. The Law of Silence will take you to greater heights than you may have imagined. It's one of the secret powers you have as a human being, so be silent!

WORDS OF POWER

In the silence of my heart, I know who I am and what I am here to do.

*Every day my soul speaks to my heart in silence,
and I listen to its wisdom.*

I take time every day to listen deeply to my soul in silence.

I am silent. I am grateful. I am present.

I sit for 15 to 30 minutes a day in silent gratitude.

I remain silent and poised.

My silence is enlightening and helps me fulfill my dreams.

MY WORDS OF POWER

_____

_____

_____

_____

_____

_____

_____

_____

MY REFLECTIONS

How can I use the Law of Silence today to fulfill my life's
purpose, dreams, and objectives?

_____

_____

_____

_____

_____

_____

_____

_____

❖❖❖❖❖

Day 10
The Law of Certainty

Imagine that you're interviewing two people for a job. Both have similar qualifications and education, and even a similar number of years of experience, but one demonstrates a greater degree of certainty than the other. You'd be wise to hire the more confident person because the individual who demonstrates the most conviction has the highest probability of accomplishing more in life and becoming a leader.

The fear and guilt that diminish certainty have stopped many people from accomplishing what they'd truly love to do—and from leading the lives they truly desire. You see, whoever has the most certainty leads and rules the game of life.

For example, I was invited to participate in a local homeowners-association meeting many years ago. There were about a dozen other people in the room, and everyone was arguing for their favorite project. There were cases made for adding sidewalks, planting trees, building a new entrance, and installing a new security system. As their arguments became louder and fiercer, I sat in silence and just listened.

By sitting there quietly, without reacting, I was perceived as having some degree of presence and certainty. When they were all finished speaking, they turned to me. Someone asked, "Well, Dr. Demartini, what do you think we should do?"

I looked at them one by one and then said, "I think we'd be wise to do all of them. The combined cost, when dispersed among all the people in the neighborhood, could easily be raised. I don't believe that there'll be any major difficulty in inspiring the members of the community to participate, since the overall appreciation in their individual property values will exceed their individual outlay. It'll be a no-brainer: We won't need to argue about the details if we just get them all done. Even if only 50 percent of our households participate, the total costs divided among us are still affordable individually."

My silence and subsequent certainty that we as a community could do it *all* inspired everybody to take action and join in agreement. We accomplished all the objectives over the next few months and added value to everyone's properties.

If you're in sales, and you have more certainty than the person buying from you does, you'll make the sale. If you have confidence in the way you present yourself to an audience, you'll rule and influence your listeners.

How can you add this quality to *your* life?

- Study the area in which you'd love to have certainty.
- Rehearse any necessary and associated skills.
- Practice acting with certainty. Play out the role. To *be,* act *as if.*

If you were to go through life imagining yourself with confidence and using your visual camera—your inner mental photography, or "mentography"—to picture yourself living as you'd love to, then you'd raise your level of certainty. Start now to affirm just how you'd love your life to be. Say to yourself, *I am certain. I know this. I am a master.* When you repeat these statements daily until all the cells of your body tingle with it, so will the world come to believe it.

Your affirmations and visualizations will build your certainty and your acts of power will add to it. What you *see* for yourself, what you *say* to yourself, and how you *act* determine your path. The Law of Certainty can be the difference between a mediocre existence and one of amazing fulfillment. You have the power to live the life of your dreams through growing in certainty.

Words of Power

I am a master of persistence. I do what it takes.
I am powerful. I am enthusiastic. I am certain.

I study truth and share my wisdom.
I study. I practice. I rehearse. I act "as if." I am certain.
I see, say, act, and know that I am certain.
As I grow daily in certainty, I live the life of my dreams.

MY WORDS OF POWER

_____

_____

_____

_____

_____

_____

_____

_____

MY REFLECTIONS

How can I use the Law of Certainty today to fulfill my life's
purpose, dreams, and objectives?

_____

_____

_____

_____

_____

_____

_____

_____

Day 11
The Law of Meditation

You may have sat in silence or meditation before. (You certainly have if you followed the recommendations I made for Day 9.) And you may already realize how valuable the art of meditation can be to those interested in creating an amazing life. If this is so, bravo! If not, this is your opportunity. Either way, today you'll review the two key components of this law: One is passive or receptive, while the other is active or assertive.

In passive meditation, you sit in total silence while you count your blessings and enter a state of deep appreciation. Then you simply remain with your eyes closed and your head and eyes facing slightly upward. In this quiet gratitude, your mind opens and allows ideas to enter; it dissolves any static and becomes clear and receptive. You become *present*.

To experience passive meditation, maintain that clear, quiet, receptive state for at least five minutes, keeping a little notepad next to you to write down any thoughts that come. You're like a radio, and you'll receive inspiring ideas in this state. When one pops up—something that you can use in your practical life—write it down and return to your meditation. Simply continue passively receiving more new guidance.

Just remember this: The more grateful you are, the easier it is to receive, and the quicker the ideas enter; the sharper the image, the clearer the message; and the more gratitude you broadcast, the more clarity you receive. If you're ungrateful, you'll become distracted, and your mind will be clouded because you'll have a lot of "static" in your receiving system. When you enter a state of *balance and gratitude,* however, the meditations become clear, and the passive reception can give you amazing insights that you'll love to write down.

Once you've received an inspiring idea, you then begin the second form of meditation: the *active* part. This means taking the new concept and immediately concentrating on it in detail, focusing and becoming completely present with it. Hold the original image of your passive meditation, and then hone in with increasing attention to the particulars. Imagine yourself creating that inspiration into reality.

You begin as a creature receiving an insight, and you end as a creator manifesting it. From passive reception to active creation: These are the two forms of meditation.

When you consciously direct your mind in this way, the ideas that are inspiring to you become part of your daily life. Apply the Law of Meditation every day. It takes only about 15 minutes in all, but it allows you to truly enter "the zone."

By that time, you become so present with your creations that they start showing up in your life. You attract the right people, places, things, ideas, and events in your mind—and make them real. Hold the images of your dreams, and apply active and passive meditation in your life. The Law of Meditation will help make your most inspiring dreams come true.

WORDS OF POWER

I love to meditate daily.

My meditation brings inspiration to my daily life.

My meditation adds to my power and fulfills my purpose.

My meditation brings action to my purpose and purpose to my action.

My meditation fills me with the power of presence.

Through meditation, I open my heart to live the inspiring life of my dreams.

Through meditation, my life increases in clarity and gratitude.

Through meditation, I focus on ever-finer detail, and my dreams manifest.

MY WORDS OF POWER

_____

_____

_____

_____

_____

_____

_____

_____

MY REFLECTIONS

How can I use the Law of Meditation today to fulfill my
life's purpose, dreams, and objectives?

_____

_____

_____

_____

_____

_____

_____

Day 12
The Law of Poise

At some time in your life, you've seen a really handsome man or beautiful woman and become distracted by their attractive appearance—you may even have become passionately infatuated. Perhaps at some other time, a car cut you off while you were driving and you became upset, angry, or resentful toward the driver. In your perception, this driver treated you inconsiderately. When you feel either infatuation or anger toward a stranger, you're not in command of yourself. Instead, your imbalanced perception of that person rules you. You don't have poise (a stable, balanced state of equilibrium), and you become emotionally off-center.

When you see more positives than negatives or vice versa, you become consumed and distracted by that distorted viewpoint. To have *presence* and *poise* (which are other words for *balance*), you must see life with equilibrium. You're bound to encounter events that at first seem terrible, but that later you'll see as actually quite fortunate. And other experiences that you first think are terrific will become terrible later. In truth, these occurrences were neither—they were always balanced—but your mind was stunned temporarily. Infatuation and resentment are blind, but a truly loving equilibrium sees the whole of life in harmony.

According to physics, every event has a balance and is neutral in its totality. That's completely true until people come along with their misperceptions and individual-value judgments. Therefore, when something occurs that you seem to be attracted to or repelled by—or when anything distracts you and takes you off-center—dig down deep inside yourself, and then go back and look at the incident with the eyes of balance.

Here's a simple tool to help you do that: Remember some event you consider terrible and think about how it has actually served you. Has it made you more accountable, wiser, more humble, or more realistic? Did it balance a misperception that life was going to be nice all the time, or that there weren't supposed to be any problems? Did it help you grow as a person? Record your thoughts on a piece of paper.

Now consider something you thought was terrific. This time, write how it was also a drawback to you, until you have a feeling of inner calm, truth, and balance. Inside every labeled "terrible" is a hidden "terrific," and within each perceived "terrific" is a secret "terrible."

Poise is healing and magnetic. It's a centering process that allows us to remain focused and avoid distractions. This state helps you accomplish your dreams and visions and gives you the capacity for leadership, no matter what the situation. If you're a victim of circumstance, it rules you, but if you're a master of circumstance and you just dance, you stay poised.

Keep a balanced perspective: Follow the Law of Poise.

Words of Power

I embrace my life's positives and negatives equally,
as two sides of a whole, and remain balanced and poised.

My heart opens in gratitude for life's balanced lessons in love.

All that happens today serves me and serves others,
regardless of polarity.

I'm grateful for the balance of positive and negative in my life.

Inside every terrible is a terrific. Inside every terrific is a terrible.
Both make up love.

I am poised and present and see the balance.

MY WORDS OF POWER

_____

_____

_____

_____

_____

_____

_____

MY REFLECTIONS

How can I use the Law of Poise today to fulfill my life's
purpose, dreams, and objectives?

_____

_____

_____

_____

_____

_____

_____

✦✦✦✦✦

Day 13
The Law of Transition

Let's say you have a job you don't love. You think, *I've got to go to work today. Blech!* You're in a desperate mode, not inspired by what you do, and your vocation and your avocation are definitely not connected. In this case, you're in one of two states: On the one hand, you may not know what you'd love to do, which is probably why you're in this situation. Or, on the other hand, you might know what you want, and you're frustrated because although you really want to do it, you don't know how. The Law of Transition provides some ideas on how to make a change from something that you don't enjoy to something that you do.

Begin by clearly defining exactly what you'd love to do. Until you know and declare it to yourself, why would the universe give it to you? Opportunity isn't going to just land in your lap if you're not willing to take some actions toward it and be clear about what you want. That's like trying to hire someone for a job description you've never defined. Just imagine trying to do that, and you'll see that it won't work.

But if you define exactly how you want your life to be, I believe that you can literally create or attract into your world the people, ideas, and events—as well as the economics—to support every imaginable job you could desire. In other words, doing what you love and loving what you do *is* possible. And you can become wonderfully paid for it.

But first, it's essential that you define it. So, sit down at your computer and type (or get a piece of paper and write) exactly how you wish your days could be spent, and the career or job that you'd be thrilled to do. Describe it fully and define it. Now go back and look at all the positions you've held, because there are no mistakes in any of them. Your previous jobs served a purpose: They gave you tools and talents that will help you in the pursuit of your dreams. Find out how those experiences were necessary, and think about how you can apply them all—please don't throw them away! Instead, build on them: How can you use those skills in this new path?

Next, start a blueprint. You might need advice from a mentor or coach during the process, but go ahead and get started developing a business-transition plan on how to enter into the career of your dreams. You may be thinking, *Well, I'm not an entrepreneur. I don't want to start my own business.* Do this step anyway, as if you were interested in striking out on your own. You may discover that you're more of an entrepreneur than you thought if you just provide yourself with the program that allows you to override fear and put contingencies in place. This step helps you conquer any doubts you may have, so develop a *plan* of *how* you could do what you desire.

A lady in Canada attended one of my personal-development programs designed to "create the career and life you dream of." She approached me and said, "Well, what I'd love to do is dance." She was a beautiful, large woman who thrived on moving to music, yet she claimed, "But I can't do that! I'm working as a secretary right now."

I told her, "Well, define how you'd love your career to be."

"I'd just be so happy to dance," she repeated, then added, "and get paid for it."

We sat down to brainstorm and begin a new business plan—and in less than one hour, we laid out a basic preliminary course and generated many creative ideas. Guess what that lady does today? She travels to various countries and organizes tours for those who want to learn unique forms of dancing from all over the world, such as Spanish flamenco, Italian tarantella, and many others. She takes people on incredible trips (sometimes 15 to 20 people or more); she charges her fee plus the price of the tour; and she spends her days dancing, traveling, and getting paid for it.

You *can* make money doing what you love and loving what you do. You must simply take the time to create and implement a plan, since transition without this step is almost guaranteed to fail. With a well-thought-out process, however, you can make the change more smoothly.

Be sure to appreciate your current job in the meantime, because it's making your new career possible. Just don't jump from your position blindly or impulsively, because that's like leaping off a trapeze without a safety net below. Appreciate what you have, and make sure that you design your transition plan. Follow the Law of Transition so that you may do what you love and love what you do.

WORDS OF POWER

I define and refine what I would love to do daily.

*I delight in defining what I love, and in planning how
I will get paid to do it!*

I see how my present job helps me do what I love.

All I do or have done is a stepping-stone to the career I love.

*I take the time to plan my life, and I am open to new
inspirations along the way.*

*My transition from where I am to where I plan to
go is running smoothly.*

I love what I do, and I do what I love.

MY WORDS OF POWER

_____

_____

_____

_____

_____

_____

_____

_____

MY REFLECTIONS

How can I use the Law of Transition today to fulfill my life's purpose, dreams, and objectives?

_____

_____

_____

_____

_____

_____

_____

_____

✦✦✦✦✦

Day 14
The Law of Completion

The more you do simple things and complete them, the better you train yourself to do what you say you will—to complete things. On the other hand, every time you set an unrealistic goal that you're not really committed to, you accustom yourself to not keeping your word to yourself. It teaches you not to "walk your talk." Each time you set goals that are higher than your capacities or values will allow—and you don't achieve them—you lower your self-worth (and you probably beat yourself up, too).

It's wiser to set goals, break them down into smaller steps with reasonable time frames, and then do them. Train yourself to accomplish what you intend to and reward yourself—then go on to the next mission and do the same. The reason most people hesitate and procrastinate is that they haven't cut their objectives down into achievable bits with proper schedules, and haven't linked each one to their highest values. When you put your goals into sensible periods of time and action steps, you tend to accomplish them and reward yourself as you develop.

Here's one that you can do today: Set the goal of drawing a perfect circle (or at least one that you're satisfied with), which is a common exercise for visual artists. If you begin drawing a circle and keep refining it until you've improved or perfected it, you'll train your brain to do what you say—to complete what you intend. Then do it again by drawing a perfect square, and later, a triangle. And then maybe some design even more complex. By doing so, you're teaching yourself to complete your objectives, which will lead to your dreams.

Patience and rehearsal make for perfection. Follow the Law of

Completion, break down your goals into smaller action steps, put them into reasonable time frames, and then reward yourself when you complete them. Train yourself to do whatever you say or intend, and watch what happens!

Of course, you must figure in one other factor: You may decide tomorrow that you have something more important to do and discard your previous plan. That's okay. Don't berate yourself over that. You haven't failed to complete your goal; you've simply clarified or upgraded it. Some of the things you don't complete are simply refinements toward higher priority pursuits, while others are incomplete because you didn't set feasible objectives with achievable schedules. Master the art of setting sensible time frames and complete what you say. It makes a huge difference in your life, and you build fulfillment for yourself. The Law of Completion is truly a key to human progression.

WORDS OF POWER

I set realistic goals that are fulfilling and that I accomplish.
I do simple things and complete them.
I break my goals down into easily doable action steps.
I set wise time frames for the action steps to my goals.
I reward myself for doing what I say.
I keep myself open to refine my plans.
I refine my priorities.

MY WORDS OF POWER

_____

_____

_____

_____

_____

_____

_____

_____

My Reflections

How can I use the Law of Completion today to fulfill my life's
purpose, dreams, and objectives?

_____

_____

_____

_____

_____

_____

_____

Week
THREE

Day 15
The Law of Greater Cause

S uppose I was standing on the corner, and I walked up to you and said, "Excuse me, I have some problems paying my bills. Could I have some money?"

You'd probably think, *I've got my own problems. Get out of here!*

Or what if I came up and announced, "You know, I've got some kids I need to put through college. Can I borrow some money from you? Will you help me out?"

You'd probably answer, "Look, I've got my own kids."

But imagine if I was to tell you, "Three years ago my wife and I had a child. Our baby was born with a deformity. We were unprepared for the massive life change this brought us, and we're still often in shock. We were beating ourselves up and wondering what we'd done to attract such a challenge. All kinds of things ran through our minds.

"Then we realized that this could be a gift. This could give us a cause to which we could dedicate our lives. We decided to create a foundation and do what we could to research this deformity—what caused it, why this might happen in families' lives, and how to prevent and treat it. As a result, we've now dedicated about 60 percent of our savings and 10 percent of our present income toward supporting this effort. Would you love to contribute in some way to try to keep children from having deformities when they're born?"

If I were to ask you that, you'd probably be more apt to contribute, because I invoked a bigger reason than just my immediate personal needs.

When your enterprise is simply yourself, you'll find few willing to support it, but if your goal involves something beyond yourself, you'll more easily find contributors. The larger your cause, the greater the opportunities you'll receive in relation to it. This applies not only to charitable organizations and ideas, but also to your personal life: If there is a greater purpose to your wealth, you'll attract greater opportunities for acquiring it.

You're also wise to ask yourself when you're developing your cause, *If I don't know what I'm going to do with the money I accumulate, why would the universe give it to me?* That is, if you'd love to make a million dollars, you need to write out what you'd do with every dollar. If you dream about $10 million, you'd record exactly what you'd love to do with every single bit of it. The same principle applies to desires for $100 million or $1 billion: Make an explicit plan for how each cent would be allocated. If you don't know what you'd do with the money and aren't sure how to manage what you'd receive, then why would the universe give it to you?

This is an important principle: Make sure you have a purpose larger than your immediate needs, or you'll become challenged in attempting to rise beyond your current circumstances. The greater your cause, on the other hand, the greater your potential wealth can be, since more people will want to support your plan, be a part of it, and invest in it.

Also, be certain that you know what you're going to do with the assets you already have. Why would you get a promotion at work if you couldn't manage the responsibilities you already had, let alone the new level of accountability? Similarly, why would you get an upgrade in wealth if you don't know how to handle what you had, let alone the new level? Those who manage money more wisely get more to manage; those who deal with it poorly receive less.

One of the secrets of this process is making sure that you have a great intention that abundance can flow to: the Law of Greater Cause. You won't find any person of vast fortune who doesn't have a larger purpose, so make sure that you plan beyond yourself.

WORDS OF POWER

I have a great cause for great wealth.

My cause is far beyond myself.

I know what I would love to do with every single dollar of my wealth.

I see each dollar of my wealth used for a cause greater than my immediate self.

It is not just about me. My purpose grows far beyond myself.

Daily, I serve others and myself.

I am on a mission.

MY WORDS OF POWER

_____

_____

_____

_____

_____

_____

_____

_____

MY REFLECTIONS

How can I use the Law of Greater Cause today to fulfill my life's purpose, dreams, and objectives?

_____

_____

_____

✦✦✦✦✦

Day 16
The Law of Discipline

This law may sound singularly uninspiring, but the word *discipline* comes from the same Latin root as *disciple.* Years ago, I sought to discover what true disciples are (as opposed to the usual meaning of "followers"), and I came to realize that these are individuals who listen to and obey the inner messages and visions of their soul. They follow their inspirations and are therefore stirred to action and focused in their pursuits: They exhibit *discipline.*

Over the years, I've asked myself, *How do I express even more inspired discipline in my life?* I knew that this was one of the keys to living an amazing and fulfilling existence. In time, I discovered that one of the ways was to use a checklist to keep me focused. It acted as a prompter to remind and even push me with questions such as: *Did I do this? Did I do that?* So I created what I call a "Did I?" checklist. What a powerful little tool it became! Every single day, I checked things off. At the time I began, I was a practicing chiropractor and kept this important list on my office desk:

- Did I read my mission statement today?
- Did I read my primary goals and objectives today?
- Did I read my affirmations today?
- Did I prioritize my actions today?
- Did I stick to my priorities today?
- Did I communicate with my clients using their terms and values today?

Everything I found to be of help in my career or life was incorporated into my checklist. Every item was written as: "Did I do that today?" Each evening, I checked them all off if I'd completed them, or put an X beside the ones I didn't do. And as time went by, I found that I was accomplishing much more of what worked by having my daily checklist in front of me.

Every morning, I looked at what I'd marked undone the night before, and at the end of each day, I saw how many checks I could get. Since the actions I'd accumulated on my list had all been proven to work, this became a way of keeping me on track and making me even more disciplined.

You may be wondering, *What happens if I'm using a checklist but I find myself still sliding on some of the actions?* Take care of this by setting up some kind of a reward system to make sure that you do what you say you'd love to do. I found a great incentive: Every time I missed one of the items on my list, I had to put $5 into a little bucket on my desk. When I did all the items on my list, my staff had to buy me lunch, but when I didn't, I had to treat them. With a large staff, this really motivated me after a while! It pushed me to do what I really desired. When you have a big enough *why,* the *how* takes care of itself. That is, if you have a large enough and inspiring enough mission, you tend to do the things that help you fulfill it.

A mentor can be another great help to you in accountability and discipline. When I was in the early years of my financial development, I found myself sometimes hesitating on contributing to my savings. I hadn't yet learned about forced accelerated automatic withdrawals into a savings account, which I now teach. If I had extra money, I only sometimes saved it—I was rather wishy-washy.

Finally, I found a gentleman who headed up a financial-planning service who helped make me more accountable. He didn't give me the option of wavering with my emotions; instead, the money was set aside no matter what—regardless of how I felt or any other distractions. That strategy worked and made me far more conscious of what I was spending and earning because it ensured that saving was a priority. If you're not disciplined on your own, get someone to make you accountable, and who will provide you with a simple strategy to follow.

These are the basics that can help you live the Law of Discipline:

- Start with a checklist.
- Give yourself rewards.
- Get someone to make you accountable.

The power of discipline will start showing up in your life. I guarantee you'll do more of what you know works, and you'll get to do more of what you love. This power makes *you* the disciple, and you get to follow your own soul—and *that's* self-actualization.

WORDS OF POWER

I read my daily checklist, and I do what has been proven to work.

I love the power that my daily checklist brings me:
It keeps me on track.

I reward myself for doing my proven priority actions.

I have someone who makes me accountable.

I am a wise and worthy disciple;
I listen to the wisdom of my soul and obey.

I am disciplined, and I am grateful.

MY WORDS OF POWER

_____

_____

_____

_____

_____

_____

_____

MY REFLECTIONS

How can I use the Law of Discipline today to fulfill my life's purpose, dreams, and objectives?

_____

_____

_____

_____

_____

_____

_____

✦✦✦✦✦

Day 17
The Law of Association

You've probably heard the sayings "Birds of a feather flock together," and "If you associate with turkeys, you end up gobbling away your days." Think about these statements. The people with whom you associate have a major influence on the way you view life.

Many years ago, I began compiling a comprehensive list of religious, philosophical, and spiritual teachers and beliefs. In my efforts to include everyone whose work is already widely known, I came across a book that summarized 3,000 religious teachings and different spiritual belief systems. At that time, I made it a priority to read something on every single one of them. I also made it a goal to travel to as many of the founding cultures as I could, meeting as many different leaders and followers of these faiths and philosophies as possible.

I did this in part because I believe that people are here to grow in tolerance, not intolerance. If you learn from and appreciate individuals from all walks of life, then you become a more global being. Associating with people from all over makes you world-wise, and spending time with those who have all types of spiritual beliefs helps you grow not only spiritually and gracefully, but also in understanding and tolerance. Contemporary philosopher and Pulitzer Prize winner Will Durant said that the greatest of religions is the most tolerant. I say that if you associate with people from all places without limiting yourself, you'll become more awakened spiritually. You're wise to look through the eyes of as many beings as possible.

Pick out great spiritual teachers and associate with them. To your amazement, you might actually be able to directly contact such founding or primary leaders. Try calling them on the phone, and you'll discover that sometimes they'll actually talk to you. Years ago, I was studying the lives and works of various Nobel Prize winners because they inspired me. I called two honorees on the phone, and I was surprised and pleased to actually talk to them. More recently, I trekked through and camped in the Himalayas (near Mount Everest), and then traveled in Nepal, where I was able to meet the Bonpo Lama, who's a leader of a tradition called the Bon religion. I had a 45-minute philosophical discussion with him about love and gratitude in the world today. How did this happen? It came about simply because I wrote down the dream, envisioned it, and manifested the opportunity to meet such spiritual masters.

Make a list of all the people you'd love to meet, all the philosophies you'd love to study, and all the ideas that would awaken your spiritual appreciation. Then go and be receptive to new associations and opportunities, and fill your time and life with such enlightened people. Perhaps you don't have the wealth accumulated to travel to meet them, but you can still look them up on the Internet or read books about their teachings and lives. Whether you interact with these thinkers in a direct or indirect way, they'll expand your spirit, for the more you fill your mind with great teachings, the more spiritually masterful you'll become.

What better actions can you pursue than those you're guided to by your wise soul? Remember: The greatest teacher, the wisest guru, is ultimately your *own* soul. If you become grateful, open your heart, and apply the Law of Association by getting together with insightful mentors, your life will unfold with even more wisdom and grace.

WORDS OF POWER

Every day, I read something that inspires me.
I listen to inspirations of great spiritual teachers every day.
I listen to the wisdom of my soul every day.
I associate with spiritually wise beings.
I fill my mind with great spiritual teachings.

My greatest teacher is my own soul's knowledge of the truth.
I am a wise and worthy mirror of my soul.
I travel the world, resonate, and associate with other great beings.

MY WORDS OF POWER

_____

_____

_____

_____

_____

_____

_____

MY REFLECTIONS

How can I use the Law of Association today to fulfill my life's
purpose, dreams, and objectives?

_____

_____

_____

_____

_____

_____

_____

_____

✦✦✦✦✦

Day 18
The Law of Self-Mastery

Mrs. Grubbs, a lovely lady who lived next door to me when I was a child, taught me a valuable lesson as I weeded my family's garden. Day after day, she'd encourage me to plant something else in the weeds' place, because otherwise I'd just keep having to come back to pull out more.

Today, I realize that a garden can be a great metaphor for a mind. Your self-mastery is determined by how well you manage your thoughts. If you plant into your mind the very fine detail of exactly how you'd love your life to be, hold that image, and feel it as if it were truly there in your inner world, you'll begin to manifest it in your life.

Your outer masterpieces will actually come from your inner self-mastery, which will require both positive and negative feedback. When it's launched, a rocket ship spends 90 percent of its energy on feedback and correction to get off the ground and into space. In your life, a high percentage of your own "launching" comes through feedback, because you require support and challenge to personally evolve. It's been shown that humans grow the most when they're right on the border of positive and negative responses.

To obtain self-mastery, you must embrace both these sides of life, as well as the full vision of your future that you hold, knowing that there will be people who like your plans and those who don't. It's been said that if you aren't being crucified, so to speak, you're not on track to ful-filling your purpose—which just means that you'll have challenges in life. That's what will make you stronger.

If you have children, for instance, and you overindulge them, they'll become weak, dependent, and insecure. If you challenge them, however, they'll grow strong and independent. So as you develop your self-mastery in life, know that whatever happens, both the positive and negative help you accomplish your mission. They're there to assist you on your path to your dreams.

Take your first step by clarifying your mission: Identify it visually until you *see* it; say it to yourself until you *hear* it; and hold it as both a thought and a feeling. Endure both positive and negative replies, for your *life* mastery is really your *mental* mastery—which is simply your willingness to embrace all aspects of your existence and not forsake your vision and focus.

The Law of Self-Mastery is yours. It doesn't cost anything except your time, effort, and focus. Right now, I ask you to *stop,* close your eyes, and enjoy the image of how you'd love your life to be. You're the master!

WORDS OF POWER

I am a master and student of persistence. I do what it takes.

I embrace all aspects of my life and maintain my vision and focus.

I take the time to focus myself daily, to see and hear my mission.

I daily plant in my mind the seeds of growth that I want in my life.

My vision and my mission manifest as I see them clearly.

I embrace the positive and the negative in the pursuit of my purpose.

I daily hold the image of how I would love my life to be.

The universe conspires to help me manifest my dream.

My Words of Power

_____

_____

_____

_____

_____

_____

_____

_____

My Reflections

How can I use the Law of Self-Mastery today to fulfill my life's purpose, dreams, and objectives?

_____

_____

_____

_____

_____

_____

_____

Day 19
The Law of Perseverance

Creative evolutionary models show us that every life-form has its time, with a beginning and an end. Likewise, everything that *you* manifest has a start and a finish. If you don't hold your vision and goals long enough, they're unlikely to materialize—perseverance is one of the greatest keys to success.

I dreamed of being a professional speaker ever since I was a teenager, and I also wanted to be involved in healing. As an adult pursuing both of these simultaneously, I hired a financial consultant, and he told me, "You know, if you stick to your chiropractic practice, you'll make the most money."

"But I'm planning on taking my practice to the world, not just to a local area," I insisted. "I'm planning on speaking to a much larger audience, bringing healing in a different form throughout the planet. I also plan on making a great income doing that."

He was unconvinced. "Well, you'll make your money in the practice. You're not going to succeed financially with speaking."

Undeterred, I countered, "I'm going to hold on to my dream. I'm not going to give up on it, because I know in my heart that this is where I'm going." I *knew!*

If you trust your intuition and inspiration, hold on to your visions, and persevere toward your goals, your dreams come true sooner or later. I hired that financial consultant 20 years ago, but he worked with me for only 4 years. He didn't last as my adviser, but I made it with my vision. Today I travel some 300 days a year, speaking around the world on healing and personal development in more than 50 countries, mainly because

I held on to my dream and didn't give up on my goal. I was unwilling to relinquish the ambitions I'd cherished since I was 17 years old.

Perseverance conquers all obstacles. Like the Law of Certainty, the Law of Perseverance is one of the grand secrets to making things happen. The person who's willing to continue—no matter what—succeeds. Consider Michael Jordan, who continually shot baskets despite what seemed to stand in his way (like not making his high school team), and persevered. He once said, "Obstacles don't have to stop you. If you run into a wall, don't turn around and give up. Figure out how to climb it, go through it, or work around it." This is the person who fulfills his or her dreams.

The Law of Perseverance involves the willingness to take action on your dreams every single day without stopping. Even if they're baby steps, each day you take another one toward your goal. The Law of Perseverance means letting neither pain nor pleasure interfere with the pursuit of your purpose. You'll be challenged in life, ridiculed, distracted, and told that you can't succeed, but pay no attention. Focus on the vision you're holding in your heart. Cling to your dream—don't lose it! The Bible says that those who lose their vision perish; I've learned that those who hold it will flourish. It's the Law of Perseverance that makes things possible and makes all your dreams come true. Never give up on yourself!

Words of Power

I trust my inspiration and intuition.
I hold on to my dreams and visions. I persevere.

I take action steps every day toward my dreams.

I let neither pain nor pleasure interfere with my pursuit of purpose.

I am a master of perseverance. I do what it takes.

It is impossible for me not to succeed, for it is my destiny.

I persevere with respect to whatever inspires me.

*It is my unique and determined form of perseverance
that keeps enabling me to succeed.*

MY WORDS OF POWER

_____

_____

_____

_____

_____

_____

_____

_____

MY REFLECTIONS

How can I use the Law of Perseverance today to fulfill my life's
purpose, dreams, and objectives?

_____

_____

_____

_____

_____

_____

_____

_____

Day 20
The Law of Self-Analysis

When I was 18 years old, I'd just returned home from a two-year surfing adventure in Hawaii to begin college. I was virtually living at the school's library each day, reading books and studying as much as I could, because I wanted to master reading. While searching the shelves one day, I came across a series of books by Mahatma Gandhi. I was impressed when I learned that he analyzed many different aspects or parameters of his life on a daily basis, writing down absolutely everything he experienced and keeping these records for later reference. I thought that if Gandhi considered this a worthy practice, then I could gain something from it, too, since he obviously had some method and reason for his actions. I looked through his memoirs to see precisely how he did it, and then I did exactly the same thing.

For two years, I recorded every single thing I did, thought, ate, and drank—and I discovered more about myself than at any other time in my life. It's absolutely amazing what you can learn if you simply do such a self-analysis. I wrote down everything I consumed and the time I did so, plus any and every physical and emotional sign or symptom, as well as any insights.

I stopped about every hour, on the hour, and reflected on what had been going through my mind: *What have I been feeling? What have I been experiencing? What did I accomplish?* I took stock of all the different aspects of what I encountered throughout the day. In the process, I discovered what truly worked for me—and what didn't. I learned about my diet, my interactions with others, fulfilling my sleep needs, meeting my reading goals, and how I could increase my learning capacities and maximize my energy levels. I found all kinds of valuable key actions that

I still use today. So many insights came from this simple exercise that I can tell you that taking the time to do self-analysis is absolutely worth it.

As you go through life, everyone else's ideas bombard you. Imagine visiting the bookstore, for instance, as I did years ago when I first started studying nutrition. I read a book and thought, *Oh! That's what you're supposed to do.* Then I read another volume that contradicted the first one. After about 20 works on nutrition, I was confused. The best way for me to understand the subject was to do my *own* self-analysis. It changed the way I ate, along with my energy level, and I have a consistent vitality today because of that personal scrutiny.

In whatever form you'd love your self-examination to take (you may want to modify what I did to fit your needs), take time every day to reflect on what you've learned about yourself. Review what you've completed or left undone; see what's working and where you're maximizing your creativity, energy, vitality, flexibility, and agility; and take note of your physical, mental, and spiritual potential.

Look at what's worked and what hasn't, because otherwise, you're left to the whims of *maybe, possibly,* and a host of other uncertainties. Anything you do that's uncertain in your life is less empowering than that which is done with certainty. The Law of Self-Analysis will add confidence to your life, poise to your body, and balance to your mind. It will help you in your relationships as you find that what you experience with others has a lot to do with what's going on inside you. This principle opens a gateway to new possibilities, so make sure that you follow the Law of Self-Analysis in your daily life.

WORDS OF POWER

I am worth the time necessary to know myself through self-analysis.

*I write down everything I do or think, and I reflect on it,
to know what works for me.*

*Through self-analysis, I more powerfully serve others
and myself lovingly.*

*I know what truly works for me because I take the
time for self-analysis.*

*I have analyzed myself to such a degree that I know how
to maximize my greatest potential.*

*I have a great mind and have used it wisely to analyze
what has worked for me in the past, so I may glean wise action steps
that will continue to work for me in the future.*

MY WORDS OF POWER

_____

_____

_____

_____

_____

_____

_____

MY REFLECTIONS

How can I use the Law of Self-Analysis today to fulfill my life's
purpose, dreams, and objectives?

_____

_____

_____

_____

_____

_____

_____

Day 21
The Law of Power

Few of us get up in the morning and think, *I wish I were weaker.* Most people dream of being more powerful and would love to have more vitality to accomplish all they'd love to do and be in life.

There are seven primary human powers. Let's explore what they are and how to unleash, increase, and develop them.

1. **Spiritual:** Having a mission—almost a sense that God and the universe are working on your team to assist you in fulfilling your personal cause or dream—brings a mystical force to everything you do. When one of my younger clients desired to take first place at her track meet, she asked, "Dr. Demartini, is there anything you can tell me that will help me become more of a winner in track?"

    I replied, "Yes! Say to yourself, *I am the vision, God is the power, and we are the team* as you run." She started repeating that affirmation to herself as she sped along the track, and she didn't just come in first—she *became* first. She awakened her spiritual power and felt she was communicating and connected with a higher source. Individuals such as Gandhi and Martin Luther King, Jr., for example, expressed this form of spiritual power.

2. **Mental:** Leonardo da Vinci is a prime example of this kind of brilliance. As people use the power of their minds, they study, learn, and develop. An expanded intellect is power in itself. Remember to use the affirmation, *I am a genius, and I apply my wisdom.*

3. **Professional:** By applying sound business principles (such as a clear vision, a strategic plan, prioritized actions, delegation of lower priorities, and feedback accountability) to your daily business life, you can garner the same prestige and influence as the heavy hitters of industry. Think of what Bill Gates has at his disposal. Whether you're a fan of Microsoft or not, you have to admit that not only has Gates amassed a fortune, but his position as one of the most successful businesspeople in the U.S. also allows him to make meaningful contributions to causes he cares about, which inspires others to do the same. Through sheer grandness of scale, he improves both his own life and the lives of millions of others.

4. **Financial:** To acquire not just wealth, but also this true power, you must pay yourself first, develop and accumulate material abundance through persistent and methodical saving, and know how to manage your finances wisely.

5. **Familial:** You'll build a dynasty through the strength of stable, supportive relationships at home. By mastering the skill of communicating your values in terms that other family members understand, you bring greater caring and respect to everybody's life. Also, being truly present with loved ones when you're home—and not being distracted by all the issues that go on in your career or the outside world—helps you remain loving and grateful.

6. **Social:** This is the power of people. The more individuals who know you and whom you know, and the more you meet and greet, the better you serve yourself. Just one example of a social powerhouse is the gentleman who owns Le Cirque restaurant in New York City: Hundreds of celebrities from around the world came to the special celebration of his restaurant's 25th anniversary. But this power can also be demonstrated by those who are far less famous: Consider the incredibly large networks that can be built through a hobby, house of worship, and volunteer work. You don't have to hobnob with the elite to amass social power; just get to know and appreciate the people around you.

7. **Physical:** You're probably already aware of the incredible allure of health and vitality. Add to that charisma and magnetism, and your physical power is enhanced exponentially. Anything you can do to heighten your attractiveness and boost your energy levels will awaken this power.

You have all seven of these powers at your disposal on some level all the time. Ask yourself where you are now, and consider where you'd love to be. Is there an area you've neglected or one you could develop? Don't just focus on a single power, or work on some to the exclusion of others, because each of them has a tremendous impact on your quality of life. Remember: Any area of your life that you don't *em*power opens the possibility that someone else will *over*power you in that arena.

WORDS OF POWER

I work at developing my seven powers of life daily.
I am spiritually, mentally, vocationally, financially, physically, familially, and socially powerful!
I am thankful that I have empowered the seven areas of my life.
My seven powers of life help me fulfill my life's mission.

I am powerful, enthusiastic, and present.
What else can I say: I am truly a power person.
I am a powerful VIP—Vitally Inspired and Purposeful!

MY WORDS OF POWER

_____

_____

_____

_____

_____

_____

_____

_____

MY REFLECTIONS

How can I use the Law of Power today to fulfill my life's
purpose, dreams, and objectives?

_____

_____

_____

_____

_____

_____

_____

_____

Week
FOUR

Day 22
The Law of Service

No matter what you do or don't do in your life, you serve, and you're worthy of love. Realize this! Somebody's gaining something in experience or benefit by whatever you do.

Imagine that you're now taking command of your ability to serve: You're directing it, concentrating it on the choices you love most, and you're on a mission to give more than others ever expected. More opportunities are coming into your life.

Make it a goal that whatever service you choose to fulfill—whichever path you find truly inspiring—you give much more than is ever expected. In fact, give twice that. This is especially powerful in business, which I learned from my own seminars. Most participants walk away saying, "Wow! I had no idea that I was going to receive so many insights in such a short period of time." I've learned that if I give them much more than they expect, they'll desire, and come back for, more.

Make a commitment to give at least 20 percent—if not 50 or 100 percent—more than what anyone supposes they'll get from you. If you work for someone else and you do this, you'll always have a job.

You'll find it especially easy to follow this principle when you open your heart and serve enthusiastically. If you're doing something that you really don't love, others can sense it. If you're pursuing something that you're truly inspired about, they can feel that, too. Your enthusiasm will add to your contributions, and those around you will desire even more.

Open your heart in service and share something of a dream you have. It's an old axiom of marketing that if you find your niche and go after it, success is a cinch. Find your specialty by discovering what inspires you most and sharing it with those who are equally motivated. Get together with anyone who's also inspired by your unique form of giving, and share your energy. Go out of your way to provide more than anyone expects, knowing that no matter what you do, you serve—and now that you've targeted your energy, maximum service comes from every drop of your life.

WORDS OF POWER

No matter what I have done or not done, I have served.
No matter what I have done or not done, I am worthy of love.
I do what I love, and I give and serve much more than what is ever expected of me.
I serve with total presence and love.
I share my inspiration with those who love the values I love.
I serve from my heart.
I love to be of service, for it fulfills me and inspires others.

MY WORDS OF POWER

_____

_____

_____

_____

_____

_____

_____

_____

MY REFLECTIONS

How can I use the Law of Service today to fulfill my life's
purpose, dreams, and objectives?

_____

_____

_____

_____

_____

_____

_____

_____

✦✦✦✦✦

Day 23
The Law of Clearance

Many people walk through their lives dragging their emotional baggage and carrying heavy burdens because of a misperceived past—events they've never broken through, seen beyond, or appreciated and loved. Just in case you're hauling around any unnecessary loads, I encourage you to do this one thing: Make a list of every single thing in your life that you resent or that you've never loved—anything that you think you made a mistake on or that you believe you could have done "better." And then go through those items one by one and ask yourself, *How did it serve me? How did it serve others?* Respond to these two questions again and again until you discover the benefits of these actions and events, and see the balance, the order, and the gifts from them in your life—and in the lives of others.

There are no mistakes: Every experience is a gift and a lesson in how to love ourselves and others more deeply. It's time to clear out the illusions you have about your past so that you can see how all events serve you—and how they help others. Keep writing about this until you can see the hidden order and blessing. Every time you reinterpret an apparently negative experience as a service—every time you can "clear" an event—you add fuel to your life rather than continuing to carry baggage and burden yourself. In other words, an *attitude* of gratitude determines your *altitude* in life.

If you go through life weighed down by resentful or guilt-filled illusions, you make yourself a victim instead of seeing and seeking your victories, so clear out the misconceptions of your past. Open yourself to the truth that no matter what you've done or neglected, you've served, and have also been ministered to.

I've been blessed to work with people for many, many years, and I've seen men and women with just about every kind of trauma, but not one event escapes this law. Look deeply and you'll see its truth.

Most people perceive superficially, but you must get below the surface and then look even further. Keep asking how every event in your life has aided you and how it has assisted others. I assure you that there's a blessing in each incident you previously thought of as a curse. There's an opportunity in every challenge. Give yourself the gift of freedom by going back in your life and asking, *How did it serve?* And, above all, love yourself.

WORDS OF POWER

Every experience is a gift.
This, too, is a gift of love.
Thank You for everything that happens. All is a blessing.
I look at both sides of every event until I see its blessing.
Love is all there is. All else is illusion.
No matter what, I am worthy of love.
I have a clear consciousness, for I have been enlightened by the truth.

MY WORDS OF POWER

_____

_____

_____

_____

_____

_____

_____

_____

MY REFLECTIONS

How can I use the Law of Clearance today to fulfill my life's purpose, dreams, and objectives?

_____

_____

_____

_____

_____

_____

_____

◆◆◆◆◆

Day 24
The Law of Alignment

Envision what would happen if the people you employ aligned their values with the mission of the company and with their job description. Imagine if the company you work for made its intentions clear and you felt personally invested in the mission statement instead of viewing it as just a bit of corporate bluster. I wonder what productivity, appreciation, and loyalty could emerge. . . .

What follows are instructions for helping you do just this using a productivity, motivation, and loyalty form. Employees and employers can fill this out to align their job descriptions with their actual work.

Begin by making five columns. The first will hold the job description, the second is blank, the middle one will give the value systems of the employee, the fourth is blank, and the fifth will have the employer's or company's mission statement.

In the first column, make a list of all the things that you do during the day, regardless of whether you like or dislike doing them. Then in the third column, put down all your values, dreams, and desires for life. In the fifth column, record your company's or employer's mission statement.

To evaluate the first column, ask yourself, *How is doing each daily action on this job description going to help me fulfill my highest individual values?* In the second column, write all the ways that the job description is assisting your fulfillment of your highest values and dreams. Keep going through every daily action on your job description, until suddenly you experience a revelation and realize, *Oh! This job is actually getting me where I'd love to go in life.*

Next, link your highest values, dreams, and goals to the company mission by asking, *How is fulfilling the mission and supporting the company's success going to help me fulfill my highest values and dreams in life?* Fill that fourth column, and don't stop until you have tears of inspiration in your eyes. When you're through with this exercise (which may take two or even five pages with all these details), you'll begin to feel grateful for the opportunity to work where you do.

You can also give this assignment to people who work for or with you. This may be its most powerful application: helping you build a team of people who're all committed to the same mission for their own highly personal reasons.

One of the most effective ways to achieve productivity, motivation, and loyalty among employees is to align their job description to their innermost values and the company mission. This doesn't mean that they sacrifice themselves for the employer, or that the business forfeits itself for the employee. It just means that their benefits overlap and align: This is the Law of Alignment. I've seen corporations literally triple their net return in less than a year from just doing this one process through all the ranks of the company. The Law of Alignment can expand your enterprise—or for that matter, if applied to your family, bring greater communication to your loved ones.

WORDS OF POWER

*I look deeper until I can see how doing my daily job duties
helps me fulfill my dreams.*

There are no mistakes. Everything serves my purpose in life.

My vocation and avocation are related: I see that they are the same.

My job and my dreams are mutually aligned.

I do what I love, and I love what I do.

No matter what the pain or pleasure, I work toward my purpose.

*I align my daily actions to my highest values and
dreams and become inspired.*

MY WORDS OF POWER

_____

_____

_____

_____

_____

_____

_____

MY REFLECTIONS

How can I use the Law of Alignment today to fulfill my life's
purpose, dreams, and objectives?

_____

_____

_____

_____

_____

_____

_____

_____

◆◆◆◆◆

Day 25
The Law of Trust

Suppose you were to believe that the world stinks, not to mention that people are crazy and hopeless. Imagine living with the perception that there are only disorders, traumas, and problems; everyone is a victim of circumstance; and there's nothing that you can do about it. You'd feel helpless and hopeless, wouldn't you? At the very least, you'd throw your hands up and exclaim, "Look at what this world is coming to!"

Do you think that such imagined perceptions would help you accomplish or fulfill what you'd love in life? Not in my experience.

Some people may say, "Well, we don't want a Pollyanna mind-set, either, where we think everything is fine and dandy and ignore the problems and issues of life." That's true, too. Both of these polarized extremes are foolish. But what about the center, the middle ground between the cynic and the idealist, where optimism and pessimism are joined? There's wisdom in trusting the world and knowing that, when united, both ends of the spectrum can meet to bring a balanced orientation and open heart.

As you read earlier, you can choose—no matter what happens, positive or negative—to extract a service, benefit, and value from every occurrence. It's wise to perceive the world as doing whatever it can to assist you in getting what you'd truly love, using both supportive and discouraging responses in a balanced fashion. When you make that leap, you'll begin to perceive the events around you differently.

Rather than blaming and making excuses, think, *I'm accountable for my reality. I have the ability to change my perceptions and become awakened to a balancing and loving world worth trusting.* A century ago, renowned philosopher and psychologist William James said that the greatest discovery of his generation was that human beings can alter their lives by changing their attitudes. I've helped thousands see their same old lives with new eyes, and watched as their experience changed from desperation and resentment into gratitude and love. Why not change *your* perception so that no matter what happens, you'll receive an opportunity to grow? You receive all kinds of responses to your actions in order to catalyze your greatness—believe that the universe is helping you. Since it isn't what happens that counts, but rather your understanding of it, why not trust the world and see that it serves us all?

Create in your mind the idea that the universe is someone worthy of trusting. Personify it and imagine it being a friend with your best interests at heart: You have a beautiful, terrible, terrific universe doing whatever it can to empower you. When you filter life through trust, amazing things happen: Instead of seeing an ordinary event as a mistake, you'll say, "What an opportunity! I know this is a gift." When you "unwrap" the matter using new, sharper perceptions, you'll discover that countless opportunities, resources, ideas, and friends can be found inside.

A few years ago I was walking down the aisle of an airplane for some in-flight exercise when I bumped into a woman. I could have just mumbled, "Oh! Excuse me," but I chose not to. Instead, I turned to her and said, "Hi, I'm Dr. Demartini. I must have been meant to bump into you today. You're obviously someone magnetic, and I must have unconsciously been destined to run into you!"

Because this turned both of our perceptions of our collision around, we struck up a conversation, and I actually ended up receiving a business opportunity out of it. This all came about because I know that there are no mistakes. There's nothing but a world trying to assist me, and I trust it.

The Law of Trust tells us to love life, and to know that no matter what happens, it's serving us. This perspective makes a difference in my life, and it can do the same in yours.

WORDS OF POWER

Universe, you are wise. I trust you.
The universe is divinely designed to teach me to love.

I trust the divine order of the universe.

Thank You, God! Thank you, universe!

I welcome all the gifts of the universe, regardless of pleasure or pain.

I balance my perceptions, seeing both benefits and drawbacks,
until I confirm the love of the universe and say "Thank you!"

All that exists is love. All else is illusion.

Positive and negative feedback help me grow. Thank you.

MY WORDS OF POWER

_____

_____

_____

_____

_____

_____

_____

MY REFLECTIONS

How can I use the Law of Trust today to fulfill my life's
purpose, dreams, and objectives?

_____

_____

_____

_____

_____

✦✦✦✦✦

Day 26
The Law of Energy

Are you running lower on energy these days? Is your vitality not quite what it used to be? Is your life today requiring you to keep up at too demanding a pace? I'm going to reveal some perceptions and actions I've discovered that sabotage people's energy, and others that build it.

If you feel drained, as if you can't get up, or as if you have chronic fatigue syndrome, know that you may be nothing more than distracted. Let's check: First, divide a piece of paper into four columns. In the first column, make a list of all the things on your mind. Whether the concerns are personal, financial, career, or health related—any area of your life, no matter what it may be—write them all down. Anything even flitting through your thoughts and taking up any space at all goes on your list.

After you've completed that, go to the second column and write down next to each item (that you listed in the first column) the name of any person to whom that corresponding action or item could possibly be delegated. Ask yourself, *Is there anyone I could give this one to?*

Often people carry tasks around in their minds, thinking, *Oh, I've got to do this. Only I can do it.* But all too frequently, they truly could entrust it to another—someone who not only wouldn't mind, but who'd be delighted to help. What about your husband or wife, or someone at work? Maybe your children, a friend, an accountant, or someone else can check a few of those items off your list. It isn't wise to desperately push yourself when you can receive assistance. Instead, it's wise to do what you love and work toward delegating the rest to others.

After you've done this, put your initials in the third column next to any item that you can't pass on—these are the things that you'll do.

Then, in the last column, write the dates that you're going to delegate or complete each of the tasks, and set realistic time frames. Many times people carry piles of *stuff* in their minds that they aren't really going to do for two or three weeks or a month—or even longer. These obligations run around in their heads, taking up space and time and distracting them. This consumes priceless energy.

When you're finished, every single item on your list will have a date on it. You'll realize, *Wow! Tomorrow, there are only a few things I have to do. Tuesday or Wednesday, I have only two tasks to take care of, and I have six on Friday.* Once they're sorted and organized in time and space (and you're able to delegate some), you won't feel as overwhelmed—and your motivation will pick up immediately.

Another strategy that can help you build your energy is to review your life again and count your blessings. Gratitude continues to be the most significant way of increasing your zest. Be grateful and keep yourself from becoming distracted from this state of mind by sorting things out, delegating, prioritizing, and putting a name and date on each task. By doing so, you won't defeat yourself with low-priority items that drain you. When you're organized and grateful, you'll rise with energy. Your fulfillment will grow, and you'll have more life—rather than just living.

WORDS OF POWER

I am energized, for my mind is clear and organized,
and I laugh at any imposing distractions.

I am focused on my daily priorities and on my purpose.

I delegate what I can. I prioritize and put a date
on what I would love to do.

I am energized, for I organize any chaos that arises in my mind.

My energy soars as I count my blessings!

I am grateful that I know some of the secrets to
living with abundant energy!

MY WORDS OF POWER

_____

_____

_____

_____

_____

_____

_____

_____

MY REFLECTIONS

How can I use the Law of Energy today to fulfill my life's
purpose, dreams, and objectives?

_____

_____

_____

_____

_____

_____

_____

_____

Day 27
The Law of Planning

You've probably heard the old adage "If you fail to plan, you plan to fail." This is just as true today as it's ever been. At 17, I learned another great morsel of wisdom from the 93-year-old gentleman who became my first mentor. He told me, "If you don't plan your life, someone else will, and you'll live someone *else's* dream."

He asked me to write a plan for my life that would last 100 years, so when I was 17, I began my Master Plan—my blueprint for living a masterful life. This mentor has since passed away, but if I could, I would certainly hug him to say, "Thank you for making such a significant difference in my life." Even today, I still refer to and refine this original Master Plan. It goes wherever I do.

What does this mean for you? *Every single day, sit and take a few moments to organize and plan your life.* Address your spiritual, mental, professional, financial, familial, social, and physical development. Put something down for each one of these major categories as you begin to outline your unique journey, your desires, and your vision.

Type your plans into a computer or write them down on paper as you take your dreams from inside your heart and make them tangible realities. There's something magical in translating abstract thoughts into recorded words—and a short pencil is better than a long memory. Sometimes you might have a jumbled idea, but when you write it on paper or type it, and really edit and refine it, your intentions will begin to crystallize and manifest themselves. You'll literally start to attract the people, ideas, and events that you hold in your mind. The *plan* helps *you* become the director of your living production.

Every day, take a few moments—even if it's only ten minutes before you go to bed or when you first wake up—to look at the map you've started. Refine it and keep fine-tuning it. I began when I was 17 years old with my aim to share my inspiring ideas with people, and to see and set foot in every country of the world. Today, many years later, that first rough draft has become reality.

You're the captain of your ship and the master of your destiny. Start with your own Master Plan: Simply take a few moments every day to draw out and design your life, just as an architect designs a skyscraper. Imagine trying to erect a building without a blueprint—the workers couldn't get anything done! You have, in a sense, all the motivated workers sitting inside you, but they can't leap into action until you follow the Law of Planning. Every day, take a quick break to keep defining and refining your Master Plan. *You're* the master!

WORDS OF POWER

Divine guidance assists me in writing my Master Plan for life.

I become the author of my life as I write my Master Plan.

*Every day I reread and rewrite my Master Plan
for the seven areas of my life.*

*Through my Master Plan, I focus daily on my
purpose and grow in doing what I love.*

I take my dreams from my heart and crystallize them on paper!

My dreams manifest as I write and see them on paper.

I refine my plans and my dreams for life every day.

My Words of Power

_____

_____

_____

_____

_____

_____

_____

My Reflections

How can I use the Law of Planning today to fulfill my life's
purpose, dreams, and objectives?

_____

_____

_____

_____

_____

_____

_____

✦✦✦✦✦

Day 28
The Law of Mental Magnitude

A young gentleman who wanted to be an international professional speaker once asked me, "Dr. Demartini, how did you develop your speaking network around the world? How have you been able to speak so frequently in so many countries?"

I told him, "Well, the size and clarity of my vision has manifested it."

"Yes," he agreed, eager for the "real" secret. "But what did you do as far as your marketing pieces? *Exactly* what did you do?"

I responded, "I don't have any marketing pieces." (I actually only had word-of-mouth marketing at that stage of my speaking career.)

He pressed, "Well, how did you expand, then?"

"Here's what I've observed," I replied. (See if you can't apply this in your life!) "In my experience, if you'd love to make a difference in yourself, you must have a cause bigger than you are. If you'd love to make a difference in your family, you must have a cause as big as your city. If you'd love to make a difference in your city, you need a cause as big as your state. If you'd love to make a difference in your state, you must have a cause as big as your nation. If you'd love to become nationally known, you must have a cause as big as the globe. If you'd love to make a global difference, you must have an astronomical vision!"

The young man then began to get the point of my message: The magnitude of your vision—the size of what you see for yourself and your resources—determines your outcome.

Sometime later, I was having dinner with a well-known mogul in the news media, and I asked him how he'd accomplished impacting the whole world. He confided that he holds a globe in his hands every morning (or he simply pictures a globe and spins it in his mind), and imagines where he wants television to come up. He holds the mental picture as if he's in outer space looking down on the planet—thinking celestially and looking terrestrially.

Most people do the opposite: They look out at space from their seemingly "small" position here on Earth. Yet this leads to little impact in life, because when you think small, your power is minimized. But if you expand yourself to the state, the nation, or the world, and start visualizing, affirming, and thinking to yourself that you're making an impact worldwide, then you'll make a bigger difference, and your contribution will expand. If you start thinking of yourself as a celestial being having a terrestrial experience, things suddenly begin to change: You attract broader opportunities from farther distances, and you become a being with global impact.

As a species, if we expand our consciousness and thinking, increasing our viewpoint of ourselves and the world, then the globe is ours—we *can* make a difference. The Law of Mental Magnitude makes that difference, so enlarge yourself!

WORDS OF POWER

I am a celestial being having a terrestrial experience.

The magnitude of the space and time inside my mind determines the magnitude of my outcome.

I see myself as an astronomical being with a global impact.

My life affects and increases the love on this planet.

I expand my thinking and my intention daily.

I have a larger-than-global vision and message, and the world is mine.

It is my destiny to impact the world.

MY WORDS OF POWER

MY REFLECTIONS

How can I use the Law of Mental Magnitude today to fulfill my
life's purpose, dreams, and objectives?

Week
FIVE

Day 29
The Law of Knowing

Psychology recognizes three levels of knowledge:

1. *Knowing* (gathering facts, intellect).
2. *Knowing that you know* (intuition).
3. *Knowing that you know that you know*
   (revealed inspiration, certainty).

When you experience illusive fear and guilt and imagine yourself going off on tangents due to unstable emotions, you're left with feelings of uncertainty. By doing so, you live in the past or the future, and you aren't loving or present. But when you're inspired and have love and gratitude, you become certain and can live in the now. Suddenly you know that you know that you know, and you have an amazing and uplifting degree of certainty.

Imagine if someone asked you right now whether you truly loved some specific person. You might be caught off guard with a feeling of uncertainty and respond emotionally by saying, "Well, I'm generally attracted to him, but sometimes I'm also repelled by him. I don't really want to live without him, but I don't necessarily want to live *with* him, either." You're uncertain, but you just sort of *know* things.

Yet if you reach a point where you go into a deeper state of love and appreciation, you can balance your perceptions of this same person and begin to know that you know how you feel. You then have a bit more certainty.

Finally, upon attaining a perfect harmony of perception, your heart opens and you have a moment of loving *presence* with this person. You're absolutely certain that you're in love: *You know that you know that you know.* Nobody can make you waver when your heart is truly open. For while imbalanced emotions make you indecisive, balanced loving lets you know that you know that you know.

Inside the human heart is a knowing that surpasses all doubt; it is the certainty of certainties. This is the Law of Knowing at its finest. It's like the unconditional love that parents have for their children. When they know that they love a child, there's no question, even though the child may do things that they like or dislike. They may be attracted or repelled, but deep inside, they know that they know that they know that they truly love that child.

Trust your intuition and inspiration, and each time your heart tells you something, act on it. Every time you become inspired, follow your insight. Train yourself to follow your heart's guidance.

Some of the greatest accomplishments and individuals come from this certainty of knowing. Great men and women have certainty and follow it. They don't doubt or waver because their certainty overrides their fear and guilt—they stay with the Law of Knowing.

WORDS OF POWER

Every day in every way I am awakening my inner heart of knowing.
I know that I know that I know.
I am present. I am certain. I am love. I am grateful.
I trust my inspirations, and I follow them, for I am certain.
My certainty overrides any fear or guilt, for I am unwavering.
My heart is my great center of knowing.
I know why I know, for my heart guides me wisely.

My Words of Power

_____

_____

_____

_____

_____

_____

_____

_____

My Reflections

How can I use the Law of Knowing today to fulfill my
life's purpose, dreams, and objectives?

_____

_____

_____

_____

_____

_____

_____

✦✦✦✦✦

Day 30
The Law of Congruency

If I'm speaking from my mind with only an intellectual perspective, it seems as if something's missing, or incongruent. But when I speak from my heart, everything seems to flow easily. Likewise, when you share something from deep inside that's truly inspiring to you, your life becomes harmonious.

When your head and your heart aren't in sync, not only does your body create disease, but your life also manifests a lack of ease. Conversely, the secret of having a congruent life—one where your actions, thoughts, and feelings work together to create a sense of effortlessness—is to make sure that you speak from your heart.

Feelings travel through barriers that thoughts alone can't penetrate, and your emotions have a power in themselves. For instance, if you say something in a monotone, it doesn't mean the same thing as it does when you put inflection into your voice, which allows a deeper meaning to surface.

I believe that there are four magical feelings: gratitude, love, inspiration, and enthusiasm. When those congruent states come across in whatever you're doing and saying, they attract people and opportunities to you. In these states, not only are your mind and physical self connected, but every cell in your body harmonizes, resonates, and magnetically draws to you the things you hold in your innermost dominant thoughts.

If you're in an imbalanced or stressful state, return to your heart, balance your perceptions, and share what you'd truly love to. People who're able to speak out and communicate a mission and a message congruently rule the world. You have the capacity to rule your life—and possibly the world to come—simply by opening your heart and sharing through the Law of Congruency.

WORDS OF POWER

I speak from my heart, and everything flows easily and congruently.

I love sharing from my heart what is important to others and myself.

My message is delivered directly from my heart.

I am grateful. I am loving. I am inspired. I am enthusiastic.

I balance my perceptions until I feel my heart open.

I am congruent when I share my inspiring words of love.

My body language is congruent, for I speak out and share my mission, vision, and message from my inspired heart.

MY WORDS OF POWER

_____

_____

_____

_____

_____

_____

_____

MY REFLECTIONS

How can I use the Law of Congruency today to fulfill my life's purpose, dreams, and objectives?

_____

_____

_____

_____

_____

_____

_____

_____

✦ ✦ ✦ ✦ ✦

Day 31
The Law of Delegation

Although not everyone has direct command over a formally structured business, this next law still applies to everyone—including parents who are in the business of managing a loving, active home: You grow in your business only as much as you can delegate.

This really hit home for me a number of years ago when I was attempting to build my organization. I wanted to do everything myself and the way I thought best, but what I was actually doing was getting in my own way. Even when I did delegate, I kept hovering over my employees to make sure that they did everything my way. I finally realized that if I wasn't going to trust them enough to release daily action steps or projects to them, then I wasn't going to be able to move to the next level in my own business.

I had to learn to delegate; otherwise, I couldn't be doing what I am today. Now I'm in my office only 15 to 20 days a year, because I'm speaking and traveling most of the time. If I had to do all the work back at my home base, I couldn't get it all done, much less have time to travel. One of the secrets of building an organization or company is to make sure that you give away the actions you're not perfectly designed and inspired to do to others who are.

There are powerful rules for this process: First, don't give someone a task that's way beyond or beneath them. That's easy to say, but not so simple to do consistently, because you must discover and fine-tune the person's skill and aptitude levels. Imagine how counterproductive it would be to give an employee a task that will burn them out by being too overwhelming for their skill level, or that will bore them because they can do far more. This sabotages not only their productivity, but also their creativity and genius. Learn to give people *just enough* of a challenge so that they're inspired and pushed to new levels, but not so much that they're overwhelmed or burned out.

I use a daily to-do list that either sits on my office desk or is stored electronically on my computer. On this form, I write all the important action steps I'm going to take care of that day. For my employees, I also create a daily delegation list, on which I prioritize everything I want to have them handle. This clarifies things for all of us. By being more concise through writing, and by giving my employees their priorities, many more important tasks get done.

When I don't prioritize the delegated items, my employees tend to do the easiest things first, and sometimes get to the most important things last—or even not at all. The lists take care of this miscommunication, and as long as the highest-priority actions get done—even if the whole list isn't taken care of—the most important goals are being met.

When you're implementing this law, make sure that you *train* your employees, *trust* them, and *release it* to them. Give them the opportunity to learn from trial and error, and don't forget to *prioritize* tasks so that they know what's most important. People who prioritize and do the ABCs before the XYZs are the ones who grow the most.

Today, there are computers, personal digital assistants, and many other devices that you can use instead of paper to communicate. I still prefer old-fashioned paperwork myself, but now I also do my writing and prioritizing by computer. Just make sure that you write down and prioritize your delegations, and *give each item to the person best equipped to do it.* Don't make anyone under- or overdo.

In addition, give your employees just enough actions so that they experience a bit of urgency. My wife and I were having dinner in Palm Beach a few years ago, and I asked a gentleman with a sizable corporation, "What's one of the secrets of running such a large organization?"

He answered, "Everything is urgent." This leader gave people just enough to keep them steadily busy so that time and space disappeared, and they were very productive.

When you're delegating, provide just enough work to keep everyone busy all day long, but not so much that they burn out. Make sure that you train and trust when you delegate, and that your employees have a sense of urgency. A mom-and-pop operation can never grow into a major enterprise without these principles, nor can any other organization expand beyond its current level. The Law of Delegation will take you much further than you could ever go on your own.

WORDS OF POWER

My inspired organization grows as I delegate more and more.

I prioritize my own daily actions and demonstrate priority working by example.

I write my daily delegations clearly and concisely, and I prioritize them for others.

I give my employees just enough action steps to challenge and support them—not too many, nor too few.

I train, trust, and release my delegations to the people best equipped to do the job.

I delegate my priorities with a sense of urgency.

MY WORDS OF POWER

_____

_____

_____

_____

_____

_____

_____

MY REFLECTIONS

How can I use the Law of Delegation today to fulfill my life's purpose, dreams, and objectives?

_____

_____

_____

_____

_____

_____

_____

_____

Day 32
The Law of Pride and Humility

Imagine that you're at work, having what at first appears to be an extraordinary day. You're elated and excited about it, almost to the point of becoming manic, thinking, *Wow! I made this. I accomplished that!* Then you suddenly attract some tragedy, challenge, or humbling circumstance that takes you off track and has you working only on low priorities. You wonder, *What on earth is going on? I was having a great day—what happened?*

There's actually a law that governs this equalizing scenario. If you allow yourself to get cocky and begin to think that you're better or more successful than you really are, then you automatically draw forces to bring you back into equilibrium. When you get overconfident, you attract challenges, humbling circumstances, and low priorities. In a sense, the universe is designed to keep you in balance and rooted in your heart. Anytime you become overexcited or manic, something arrives to calm you down.

On the other side of the coin, if you get blue, depressed, or frustrated; beat yourself up; or think that you're less than you truly are, then someone usually comes along and supports you. They make you laugh and build you up with pride, saying, "Hey! You're better than that!" They bring you back to equilibrium and get you realigned with high priorities.

In other words, when you're *down* and out, you attract assisting forces to build you up and in. When you're cocky and *up* and think you're greater than you are, you attract resistant forces that humble you down. You're here to be true to yourself in balance. Nature works on your behalf with positive and negative feedback to help you hone in on—and keep your heart open to—love. The world ever pushes you to do what you love and love what you do.

Maybe you've tried to (or wished that you could) stay positive and be "up" all the time. I spent years attempting this—to be a one-sided magnet—but I didn't find that approach to be most productive in the long run, as I discovered how well the Law of Pride and Humility really works.

Public optimists often become private pessimists, downloading their negativity onto the people they love most in order to look good out in public. The secret is not to get elated or depressed, because if you allow yourself to become too high up, you'll find yourself too far down. Eminent psychologist Abraham Maslow said that self-actualization is a synthesis, a perfect blend of both pride and humility.

Those who are self-actualized—who are masters, going places, and doing what they love and loving what they do—are the ones who know how to bring these two sides of themselves together and don't permit themselves to get too high or too low. Financial wizard Warren Buffett warns that you'll never manage your wealth until you manage your emotions. I can add to that: You won't manage your *life* until you manage your emotions. Stay focused and centered in your journey, and follow the Law of Pride and Humility all the way to your heart and dreams.

WORDS OF POWER

Thank you for all that brings my life to perfect balance.

*Thank you, nature, for forever pushing me to do what
I love and love what I do.*

My life is a combination of pride and humility joined together.

I bring my highs and lows into balance with gratitude.

*I balance my elation and depression. I look for the other side until
I see and feel the truth of love.*

I let neither an up nor a down interfere with my dreams.

I take neither credit nor blame. I just stay focused on my aim.

My Words of Power

_____

_____

_____

_____

_____

_____

_____

_____

My Reflections

How can I use the Law of Pride and Humility today to fulfill my
life's purpose, dreams, and objectives?

_____

_____

_____

_____

_____

_____

_____

_____

Day 33
The Law of Stability

No doubt you've become highly agitated at times, and you may have even considered yourself to be an emotional basket case during some moments. Other times, you've been quite stoic and stern, more cognitive and intellectual, and didn't waver easily. Halfway between those two extremes is what I call the center point underlying the Law of Stability.

Many times in a marriage or long-term relationship, one spouse or partner will play the cognitive role, while the other is the connotive. The cognitive person thinks things through without considering his or her emotions. The connotive one doesn't rely on thinking, but simply feels everything and bounces around like a Ping-Pong ball. Stability is where these forces of thought and feeling, of mind and heart, come together and are united. When you're in such a balanced state, you have equilibrium of all these aspects and are neither elated nor depressed; you're centered with love.

Stability is demonstrated when you have a clear mission—a focused vision and plan of action—certainty about where you're going, and caring feelings that inspire you as you align yourself with what's most purposeful. You're not simply a cognitive intellectual, nor are you emotionally incapacitated. You're in balance and feel harmony with all creation, doing what you love and loving what you do. This is called "stability."

Anything that isn't centered attracts something that brings it to that point. Therefore, you grow in your stability as you mature. In fact, becoming mature *is* stability. If you have frequent emotional ups and downs, don't be surprised if a plethora of stoic people turn up in your life as time goes by. They're simply there to teach you how to bring yourself to equilibrium.

The art of living by this law involves the willingness to embrace both sides of yourself and enter your heart. Bring heart and mind into every action of your life, and watch what happens: You'll attract different relationships, wealth, and opportunities, and train your spirit in gratitude. The secret of this law is the centered union of both mind and heart—by balancing them, you apply the Law of Stability.

WORDS OF POWER

My mind and heart are one, and my wisdom and love are at the center.

*I abide by the wisdom of my mind and the love of my heart,
and I fulfill the life of my dreams.*

I am stable, for I listen gratefully to my mind and heart.

*I bring my mind down to my heart and my heart up to my mind, and
listen to their guiding inspirations.*

I have a clear mission, a clear vision, and a clear plan of action.

I am stable and unwavering, for I know my heartfelt destiny.

MY WORDS OF POWER

_____

_____

_____

_____

_____

_____

_____

_____

MY REFLECTIONS

How can I use the Law of Stability today to fulfill my life's
purpose, dreams, and objectives?

_____

_____

_____

_____

_____

_____

_____

_____

✦✦✦✦✦

Day 34
The Law of Wealth Appreciation

If you'd love to build your financial fortune, read this chapter carefully. After interviewing and consulting hundreds of individuals with varying degrees of wealth, I've found that those who recognize what money represents and what it can do—those who appreciate the ability to manage or receive and give wisely—are those who build wealth. I've also talked with people who have very little income or wealth, and they say, "Well, I'm really not in it for the money. Money isn't important to me. That's not why I do what I do. If I make some cash, great, and if I don't, I'll do this anyway."

The people who have wealth are those who're able to say, "I have a cause for it. I know how to manage it. I desire to build wealth. I have something significant to do with it." They appreciate and value their opportunity to build wealth and their ability to use money for fair exchange. They discuss it, study it, and put some energy into it. They know that they're responsible for what they do with it, and they love that responsibility.

If you don't appreciate something, why would it come into your life? Imagine this: You're in an art gallery, and the artist is standing near his or her work. You walk up to the display, then shrug nonchalantly and walk away. What do you think that artist will do? Do you think that he or she will be inspired to create another painting? Probably not, if everyone acted just like you. But what would happen if you saw the piece and appreciated it, saying, "Wow!" and gathering all your friends to admire it? That would probably inspire the artist to create another masterpiece.

The same is true in life: If someone has given us a gift, and we're thankful, we're likely to receive more gifts. The blessing of wealth likewise goes where it's appreciated.

If you don't fully embrace the ideas of saving, spending, managing, and dealing with money wisely, or acknowledge what it can do and how it can serve people, then don't expect to have much wealth in your life. One of the most important things you can do, if you expect to have any prosperity at all, is to learn to appreciate what it can offer. In strong hands, it can be used for powerful purposes—for positive or negative effects. Wealth itself is neutral until someone employs it and projects a valued intention onto it.

Here's a great way to enhance your wealth appreciation—and, therefore, your abundance potential. Sit down and write 100 reasons and 100 benefits outlining how money coming into your hands could help you and the world. Then write another 100 things that you can do with it. If you don't know how you're going to use it, why would it come to you? Be thankful for a wealthy life. Appreciate the opportunity to manage wealth, and watch *it* appreciate in your hands. The Law of Wealth Appreciation can build you a lasting fortune.

WORDS OF POWER

I appreciate the value of money and what it can do for the world and me.

I study, work toward, and put energy into building my financial empire.

I am writing 100 benefits describing how wealth in my hands can improve the world and myself.

Wealth comes to me because I appreciate it.

Wealth comes to me because I have a cause for it that is greater than myself.

I am given wealth in many forms. I appreciate all of them. Thank you.

I am a multimillionaire money magnet who appreciates the value of wealth.

My Words of Power

_____

_____

_____

_____

_____

_____

_____

_____

My Reflections

How can I use the Law of Wealth Appreciation today to fulfill my
life's purpose, dreams, and objectives?

_____

_____

_____

_____

_____

_____

_____

_____

Day 35
The Law of Wellness

Most people live with a myth—the myth of health. Let me explain: I differentiate between wellness and health. Every single day within your body, cells are dying and cells are being born. Your skin, intestinal, and lung cells are changing constantly, and the other cells of your body are turning over on a regular basis. In other words, you literally become a new person as days go by, since your body is constantly evolving. It's both destructive and constructive, and all transformation depends upon this cycle.

Most people think, *Well, I just want to be healthy, and I don't want any disease or death.* The reality is that you experience both life and death all along your earthly journey. Throughout your life, you're made of cells that are sick and dying, as well as ones that are being born and growing. *Wellness* is embracing both sides of that—health is just one aspect, but most people are infatuated with it and are resentful of disease. Whenever they have any sign of illness, they beat themselves up and think that there's something wrong with them.

You don't want to be in a fantasy that you'll be healthy all your life and experience nothing else. If you're infatuated with that, then when you're in your later years (or whenever the body begins to accelerate its breakdown), you'll resent yourself for undergoing such a natural process. I say embrace both health and disease, and wellness is yours.

That doesn't mean that you should ignore any efforts to help maintain your body's optimal evolvement—you should absolutely eat, drink, and exercise well. What I *am* saying is this: Do more than just accept the inevitabilities of life; *embrace* both the building and the destroying.

You're constantly remodeling and re-creating yourself, like a large city always under some construction. A part of you catabolizes and breaks things down, and another part anabolizes and builds things up, and thus you achieve metabolic equilibrium, which needs both sides. A wellness program isn't enamored with one and resentful of the other, but welcomes both.

I did a survey in which I asked the subjects to write down every sign and symptom of disease or disorder that they were aware of, or that someone else had acknowledged in them. Everyone has these—red eyes, dandruff, uneven skin pigments, gum disease, aches, and pains. We all have these signs of life's wear and tear, so why flog yourself if you're beginning to "age" a little?

Health *and* disease make up wellness. When you run from one and seek only the other, you have a neurotic *illness,* which disowns half of you, while *wellness* embraces all. Someday when you're 90 or 100+ years old, your body is going to decide, "Okay, that's enough." It's just part of the game, and you'll fare better by appreciating both sides. Otherwise, you'll be anxious much of the time and living in a fantasy about how your body is supposed to run.

Be grateful for your physical self and whatever it does for you, as ultimately it's teaching you how to love. Every sign and symptom is just trying to impart this one lesson: Love both sides of your wellness.

WORDS OF POWER

I am grateful for my body and for whatever it does for me.

I embrace both health and disease as the two sides of my wellness.

Every sign and symptom of disease or
health is teaching me how to love.

Both health and disease teach me the wisdom of love.

I see all transformational changes in my body as a state of well-being
as I progress toward God in love.

I am a human transformer:

*I both build and destroy and build and destroy
and build and destroy my lovely body.*

MY WORDS OF POWER

MY REFLECTIONS

How can I use the Law of Wellness today to fulfill my life's
purpose, dreams, and objectives?

Day 36
The Law of Growth

I think of life as a tree: As a tree grows, its little green sprigs reach out to get as much of the sun as they can, to acquire greater respiration and life. The branches that don't aggressively push themselves toward the sun become shaded over, and they eventually die and fall off.

As you grow, you may shed "leaves," as well: friends, acquaintances, and colleagues. And you'll build new friendships as you drop the old ones all along your journey of life. Yet you may be afraid to discard your past, and instead hold on to those around you, when you really need to let go and move on.

Those who start out "in sync"—sharing the same level of ambition or having common goals and interests—may find that they've diverged sometime later on. We all have plateaus in life when it's best to stay put, just as we all have periods of intense drive and focus. It's important to recognize when you've fallen out of sync with someone. If you want to expand and go further in life, you may have to leave behind some of those less ambitious people who aren't willing to continue to grow—at least not in the direction that you desire to. It's wise to associate with individuals you resonate with, those who are where you'd love to be.

Sometimes people let their fears block progress and imagine that they're going to lose their best friends. But do you hang out with all the same people who went to elementary school with you? Probably not. What about high school and college buddies? Even here, I'm guessing it's very few, if any. How about co-workers from your first job? You get the point: As you think back, you'll see that you've shed many people throughout your life, so don't be afraid to do this. It isn't necessarily putting people down, but simply allowing yourself to grow.

If you're having difficulty letting go of a relationship, remember that you may greatly honor yourself and the other person by allowing both of you to evolve. You don't serve the world by shrinking, but by shining and allowing others to have their freedom—as you set *yourself* free by developing and becoming the person you're truly capable of being. By doing this, you give others permission to do the same.

Be willing to let go and thrive. As long as you're green, you're growing, but as soon as you're ripe, you'll rot, so allow the Law of Growth to rule your life. Let yourself shed your leaves and sprout new ones. You may have to rake occasionally, but with every spring comes a new surge of glorious growth.

WORDS OF POWER

I associate with those who support and challenge my values perfectly— those I presently resonate with—and I shed the rest.

I gratefully let go of relationships that are lower on my priority list and that dissuade me from living my deeper purpose in life.

My friends change naturally as I grow and change.

I love to share my life with people who are inspired by my purpose.

I am like the great tree of life, forever reaching for the sun and shedding my unproductive leaves along the way.

I love spending time with people who help me grow in love.

MY WORDS OF POWER

_____

_____

_____

_____

_____

_____

_____

_____

MY REFLECTIONS

How can I use the Law of Growth today to fulfill my life's
purpose, dreams, and objectives?

_____

_____

_____

_____

_____

_____

_____

_____

Day 37
The Law of Refinement

Some of the earliest mediums of economic exchange were heads of cattle; in fact, the word *capital* comes from that—*capita:* "heads of cattle." However, if you were out of fair exchange in those early days and you owed "money" to someone, the animals were large and difficult to divide and use as pay. To offer a reasonable barter, using half a cow, or a quarter (unless you were a butcher in the meat market) posed a significant challenge and was cumbersome, to say the least. Little by little, economic exchange became refined, evolving into coins, paper, plastic, and eventually an electronic medium. Now money exchange has become expressed in the most efficient form yet, and sophisticated economic transactions are completed at the speed of light.

Likewise, your individual personal development and financial management go through refinement as you mature, so if you have a dream and a mission for life that's boiling inside and that you'd love to fulfill, it's wise to write it down. You'll begin with a general written mission statement, but after you reread, review, and rewrite it periodically—just as in economics—you'll finally refine your statement of purpose into a masterpiece.

I encourage you to take time every day to look at your dreams, mission statement, and values, and constantly refine them so that you can become enlightened. With this process, you make a commitment to yourself: *I am here to become a master of refinement. Every day, in every way, I am becoming more refined.*

Through this alchemy, the raw metal of your being becomes the refined gold of achievement and mastery. Follow the Law of Refinement and watch the transformation begin.

WORDS OF POWER

I write what I would love to accomplish, and I refine it daily.

I look at my dreams, my mission statement, and my values, and I keep refining them.

I am a refined being building a refined life as I become enlightened.

I am evolving my raw minerals into refined precious gems.

I am a masterpiece of refined art, sculpted by my inspired soul.

MY WORDS OF POWER

_____

_____

_____

_____

_____

_____

_____

MY REFLECTIONS

How can I use the Law of Refinement today to fulfill my life's purpose, dreams, and objectives?

_____

_____

_____

_____

_____

_____

✦✦✦✦✦

Day 38
The Law of Visualization

About 15 years ago, as I was walking through the Galleria shopping mall in Houston, I entered the American Express Travel service center and requested a copy of every brochure they had.

The travel agent looked up at me and asked, "*Every* brochure? Can't you be more specific, sir? Do you have a particular destination in mind?"

I answered, "No. I want to see every one you've got. I'm going to lunch, and I'll be back in about 45 minutes. If you could have every brochure your company has ever produced all together for me, I'd really appreciate it."

When I came back, she had almost a solid foot and a half of stacked brochures waiting for me. I brought my dolly cart and wheeled the whole pile over a skywalk to my private office in an adjacent building. Once there, I cut out every picture of all the sights I'd love to see around the world: extraordinary and beautiful places, from Egyptian pyramids to the Tibetan palace to the Great Wall of China—from the Eiffel Tower to the Acropolis to the Vatican!

I put all these pictures in a folder, and every day at the office, I'd take a few moments and look through them all—hundreds of photos of places I'd love to visit. I disciplined myself to visualize being there, and in the 15 years since this occurred, about 65 percent of those destinations have materialized in my life. Mysteriously, someone called me from Rome to say, "Dr. Demartini, we'd love for you to come do a program here," and I was able to visit the Vatican! Someone else contacted me to ask, "Can you take us on a trip to Egypt?" I put together a book on Egyptology just to study it so that I could go to that country, and sure enough, I got *paid* to tour all the ruins of the ancient pyramids and temples.

Of all the places in my life that I visualized, beginning with just a picture, 65 percent of them have been completed. I've been to, spoken at, or somehow become involved in and visited the sites I've visualized. One is a beautiful Greek-inspired piece of architecture outside the San Francisco area. I got the request, "Can you speak at our wedding?" and there I was, working in that magnificent location.

I have no explanation other than the power of visualizing where you want to be (and how you'd like to get there), which makes a huge difference. A friend of mine in a large multilevel organization told me that he was taught to envision his dreams—his ideal house, car, and life. Over the course of five years, I watched this gentleman go from barely making ends meet to being at the top of his company and achieving each of those goals. The power of visualization is astounding and will lead you to an amazing life.

Every day I spend at least a few moments picturing my outcomes. I imagine myself out in space looking at the Earth, and I ask myself, *Where would I love to go? How would I love my life to be?*

Imagine *yourself* from a celestial perspective looking terrestrially. If you do so, and visualize your journey the way you'd love it to be, then your life will turn out that way. This process is one of the key elements in creating your extraordinary destiny, so apply the Law of Visualization every day. Watch your dreams come into being as you mold your life the way you've dreamed.

WORDS OF POWER

Every day I visualize exactly how I would love my life to be.
Daily I see myself living the life of my dreams in ever-finer detail.
My life becomes the dream that I see in my mind and feel in my heart.
As I clarify my vision, my dreams emerge and materialize in my life.
I see how I would love my life, and my life of love comes into being.
I can live the life I love. I can live the life of my dreams. I am thankful.

MY WORDS OF POWER

_____

_____

_____

_____

_____

_____

_____

_____

MY REFLECTIONS

How can I use the Law of Visualization today to fulfill my life's
purpose, dreams, and objectives?

_____

_____

_____

_____

_____

_____

_____

✦✦✦✦✦

Day 39
The Law of Equilibrium

Many centuries ago, a great philosopher said that the will of God is equilibrium. In ancient spiritual writings, it's shown that those who are proud will be lowered, and the humble will be exalted—mountains will eventually be eroded and leveled, and valleys filled. This is the Law of Equilibrium, and it holds true in every aspect of your life.

Consider the most traumatic and terrible events you've experienced, perhaps when someone criticized you or when you had excruciating pain, and ask yourself, *Exactly at that moment when someone was putting me down, who was lifting me up? At the precise time that someone was criticizing me, who was praising me? At the second something terrible was occurring, where was something terrific taking place?* If you look carefully, you'll see that the Law of Equilibrium held true, and that one-sided events are illusions of selective attention.

What's the significance of this? Are you meant to be only neutral and not have any reaction at all in life—or are you possibly guided to love and embrace both sides of your reactions to life? Let me give you an example involving a famous musician: At one of his greatest performances, where he received the largest standing ovations of his life, his most tragic event simultaneously occurred. Another famous entertainer also had his greatest presentation just as he learned that his best friend was dying of cancer.

At the exact point when you have your peak experience, there's also a trough, but this isn't meant to discourage you, as you may first think. Rather, this law can inspire you and keep you centered and present within your heart. You're not here to get elated, depressed, proud, humiliated, manic, depressed, infatuated, or resentful. Instead, it's your purpose to live in equilibrium and be poised, gracious, loving, and grateful for life.

The Law of Equilibrium is another expression of the Law of Gratitude, for when you possess perfectly balanced emotions and perspective, it's impossible not to be grateful and filled with true love as you see harmony and embrace both sides of life. The greatest discovery of the human experience is that no matter what happens, it will always even out, for all events come in pairs of opposites. You don't—and can't—cause or prevent this; it simply *is:* praise and reprimand, peace and war, positive and negative, support and challenge, attraction and repulsion.

Nature always provides experiences that reveal your heart and soul's mission and purpose. Since the Law of Equilibrium is one of the greatest spiritual principles, make sure that you see it as part of your life. Rather than limiting yourself to a selectively exclusive attention to either the terrible or terrific, keep an eye open for both sides of every event, for all things are neutral until you judge them not to be—they're simply messages of love.

WORDS OF POWER

All events in my life are balanced and simply messages of love.

I am not here to be happy or sad, only to understand and embrace the truth of love and equilibrium.

I am centered and poised, for I embrace the positives and negatives in equilibrium.

The balance of ups and downs in my life centers me in my heart of love.

Pain and pleasure, praise and reprimand, support and challenge— are all in equilibrium.

My will is in equilibrium, and therefore I am free.

MY WORDS OF POWER

_____

_____

_____

_____

_____

_____

_____

MY AMAZING REFLECTIONS

How can I use the Law of Equilibrium today to fulfill my life's
purpose, dreams, and objectives?

_____

_____

_____

_____

_____

_____

_____

Day 40
The Law of Mind-Body

You've almost certainly heard and read about the idea that the mind and body are interconnected. When I first began studying healing processes more than 30 years ago, certain factions in the medical community were debating whether the mind and psychology had really anything at all to do with the body and healing. And at the time that I was 18 years old and just beginning to learn about psychosomatic illnesses, there were only a handful of diseases that came under that course of study. Today, however, there are more than *100* different physical conditions known to be influenced by the mind, and psychoneuroimmunology is a huge field now. There's no way to deny anymore that your mind and body are related.

It's my experience that if you have an imbalanced perspective on life and are infatuated, resentful, elated, or depressed about some event, it's impossible to be in that emotional state without also having a physiological reaction and response to it. In fact, if someone were to tell you that a stove is hot, and you then put your hand on it, your nerves would probably prepare to burn. In some studies, it's been shown that if subjects are blindfolded and told that they're going to hold a hot poker, but instead an ice cube is placed in their hands, most people actually burn and create a blister from the expectation of heat alone.

Your perceptions affect your body, and if you have *imbalanced* perceptions, you'll have a physical over- or underreaction, which creates disease. Your entire being responds to emotions: Garbage in, garbage out; balance in, wellness out.

If you have emotions of fear and guilt, you may produce disease.

That's the beauty and magnificence of nature: It does whatever it can to teach you where you're off-kilter by giving you feedback with each sign and symptom. These clues show where you're misunderstanding equilibrium and seeing incongruity. Disease isn't terrible; it's an essential guide, for the mind-body connection works so that you can grow in gratitude and love—the two greatest wellness promoters in life. You can't find anything more powerful than that.

The body and mind are inseparable in their interactions. Keep this in the forefront of your thinking whenever you perceive a troubling sign or symptom, and look inside yourself rather than blaming something outside. Be accountable and see what in your psychology may be affecting you. If you change your perceptions and bring yourself to balance, gratitude, and love, your body takes care of itself in accordance with the Law of Mind-Body.

WORDS OF POWER

My gratitude and love make me whole and return me to wellness.

*I am aware that changes in my mind and body act
as messengers of love and truth.*

*I can change my body by changing my mental
perceptions.*

*My mind and body are gifts from my soul that guide me to
wholeness and wellness.*

*All that happens in my mind and body guides
me toward my mission of love.*

Thank you, body-mind, for serving my soul.

MY WORDS OF POWER

_____

_____

_____

_____

_____

_____

_____

_____

MY REFLECTIONS

How can I use the Law of Mind-Body today to fulfill my life's purpose, dreams, and objectives?

_____

_____

_____

_____

_____

_____

_____

✦✦✦✦✦

Day 41
The Law of Caring

Most likely there's someone you care about deeply, but sometimes your idea of trying to show your devotion is misinterpreted. Maybe you've done something that you consider loving (such as giving flowers), but the other person has questioned your intentions or wondered about an ulterior motive. The Law of Caring provides some wonderful guidelines for giving and loving in ways that are difficult to misunderstand.

First, let's start with a definition of *caring:* It's the ability to honor another individual deeply enough to know what their principles are and convey your beliefs in terms of theirs. In other words, you'd be wise to communicate with regard for your loved one's highest values—whatever is most important and valuable to *them.*

The following story illustrates this idea: A married man once sent his wife to me for a consultation because he felt that she needed to change her ways. In his mind, she was wrong in some of her views and manners. Although I normally prefer to work with the person who desires the change, in this case the husband wasn't receptive or available. So I met with his wife, and we spent the day working on his objective. Yet I didn't try to change her—instead, I spent the day *teaching* her how to communicate her needs and priorities in terms of his. I had her write down all his highest values, which included golf, business success, making money, looking good, driving fast cars, and spending time with friends. Then she listed hers: time with her children, seeing her family, looking good, fixing up the home, and so on. When she finished, I had her role-play her communications with him, and she practiced conveying what was most important to her in terms of what mattered to him.

When she returned home, their whole relationship shifted. In fact, I received a thank-you letter from the husband, saying, "Whatever you did with my wife, it truly made a difference!" What I *really* did was spend the whole day showing her how to get whatever she wanted from him—and he was thanking me.

She learned and reflected, and then honored him enough to know what his values were. She began to think out in advance (before she spoke) how to communicate her desires in terms of his priorities. For example, when she wanted to go overseas to visit her mom in Europe, she put it this way: "Honey, I believe that right now there's a sale on in Europe, so if I went over there, the amount I could save getting discounts would cover the cost. It wouldn't even cost us anything [his value of conserving money]. And I know that you have a very busy golf tournament coming up. This way you could be left alone and really have an enjoyable time with your buddies [his value of golf and spending time with his friends], and I could get the shopping done—and save at the same time." She communicated in terms of his values so that she could fulfill her own.

Just as there's an art of communication, there's an art of caring, and when you follow it, you'll receive more of what you want. You'll get more out of your relationships and be able to experience the true love that you've desired. The Law of Caring works, so communicate your values in terms of those of the ones you cherish, and just watch what happens.

WORDS OF POWER

I care about the people I love, and discover what is important to them.
I honor others and myself by communicating
my values in terms of theirs.
I love to care for others by seeing the congruity between our values.
I respect and serve others and myself by caring
sincerely and honoring all our values.
I express what is important to me in terms that are important
to them, and our mutual needs are thus fulfilled.

MY WORDS OF POWER

_____
_____
_____
_____
_____
_____
_____
_____

MY REFLECTIONS

How can I use the Law of Caring today to fulfill my life's
purpose, dreams, and objectives?

_____
_____
_____
_____
_____
_____
_____

✦✦✦✦✦

Day 42
The Law of Reflection

Years ago I began to pay close attention to what I was saying to others and what I was seeing in them. I noticed that what I said, especially in teaching, was really also meant for me, and that what I saw was a reflection of me. If I were in a particular mood, I noticed that other people were, surprisingly, also in that mood. Yet I wasn't influencing them; it was just that in observing, I was more inclined to notice a mirror of *myself* than anything else.

One day I went through the large Webster's dictionary and took an inventory of all the possible traits a human being could have. I circled them, and over a period of months, I went though every single one and asked myself, *Where do I have that trait?*

This was one of the most revealing experiences of my life because it made me realize that I had every single attribute. I looked at nice characteristics, along with mean, honest, and deceiving ones; as well as times when I was friendly or not, when I'd tried to get something for nothing, and when I attempted to be altruistic and give something for nothing. It amazed me to find all of them in myself, because I had a tendency to want to only see the good. Yet with honest self-examination, I found that I had both the positive *and* negative—which were ultimately neither.

I also realized that every facet helped others and me: Sometimes when I wasn't so nice (or was even mean), the person would come back and tell me, "Thank you! You know, when you acted that way, you really made me think and reflect, and I decided to shift my life because of it." In this way, I found that some of the things that I didn't like about myself were actually serving others, and finally acknowledging this fact was one of the most liberating experiences of my life. Freedom from fear and guilt is priceless.

I like to think of myself now as both virtuous and vicious, saint and sinner, nice and mean, arrogant and humble, generous and selfish, positive and negative. I embrace both my light and shadow sides, and I encourage you to do the same. After all, you can't run away from half of yourself. You'll never find *ful*fillment trying to do so, but will only reach "half-fillment."

The truth is that *you* have both sides, just like me, and you don't have to run from that awareness. You're still worthy of love, because every part of you contributes to the world. Every day, say to yourself, *No matter what I have done or not done, I am worthy of love. No matter what I have done or not done, I have still served.* By doing this, you'll shift your life, and you won't have to carry around so much baggage of fear and guilt.

Understand that this isn't an excuse for you to gloat, "Well, I can get away with doing anything!" That isn't the point. You already act in a variety of ways, and all you can do is change the form of your traits to work more effectively according to your evolving values. If you think, *I'm not going to be mean anymore,* your meanness will just change its form. You may become spiteful at work, bad-tempered with your children, or harsh to yourself. Somehow, you have every trait—and always will. They stay with you for life, so love them all and let them serve you and the planet.

The Law of Reflection makes you realize that you have whatever qualities you see in others; they're just manifested uniquely within you according to your own values. If you understand that, then there's nothing to condemn about anyone else, and you're free of self-righteousness. Being judgmental isn't going to make you feel loved, but learning how to reflect and find in yourself what you see around you will open the door to your heart and allow more love into your life.

WORDS OF POWER

I have every trait, both positive and negative,
and all my traits serve the universe.

I embrace my light and my shadow sides,
for all my traits are parts of love.

What I see in others, I also see in myself in some form.
I share the same traits as everyone else, and they share mine.
Whatever I see is my reflection, and I am learning to love it all.
I love what I see, for it is me.

MY WORDS OF POWER

_____

_____

_____

_____

_____

_____

_____

MY REFLECTIONS

How can I use the Law of Reflection today to fulfill my life's
purpose, dreams, and objectives?

_____

_____

_____

_____

_____

_____

_____

Day 43
The Law of Application

About 15 years ago, I was presenting a seminar in Houston called "The Breakthrough Experience." A gentleman in his 70s was there, and he stood up on the second day and asked if he could make a brief presentation to the small, private group of about 15 people. We all agreed, and he began, "I'd love to share a story about how important it is to follow these laws that you teach. Forty years ago I was attending a seminar with a group of people just like this one, except the instructor was Napoleon Hill."

Most of us knew that Napoleon Hill was one of the legendary teachers of personal success, so we were excited to hear from someone who'd seen the master at work. Most of the students in my classes—and many of the most successful people in the world—have read his books and been inspired by his teachings.

The gentleman continued, "Dr. Demartini, what you teach is very similar to Napoleon Hill's wisdom. I'd like to share with you the story of what he did for me. Four decades ago he asked the class I was in to write down our mission statements, our chief aims in life. We were also to write our goals and our auto-suggestion affirmations. At that time, I wrote on a little piece of paper the dreams that I had for my life, and my chief goals."

He pulled a yellow, taped-up piece of paper from his wallet and read the contents to us: "I'm to be a multimillionaire. I'm to have a big mansion in Houston, Texas. I'm to be the headmaster of my former university. I'm to have a luxurious Mercedes. I'm to have a wonderful, huge corporation employing lots and lots of people. I'd love to have a beautiful wife. I'd love to have two children."

He went down this list of all the dreams he'd love, and as he was speaking, a tear came to his eye, and he said to the group, "Every one of these things has come true. I have that beautiful home. I have that beautiful wife. I have those two gorgeous children. I became headmaster of my former university. I've had that huge corporation. I have that beautiful car. Everything on that list has come true." And then he continued, "And today, it's so appropriate that I'm here   because the final thing on that list, the thing that I've always wanted to create, was a book on how to turn mom-and-pop operations into major corporations."

He reached down into his briefcase, and he pulled out the completed manuscript of his new book. He told us, "The reason I wanted to stand up today is to let you know that it's great to be able to accomplish these goals, but what's more significant to me is that I'm sitting down today and writing the script for my next 40 years! As Napoleon Hill taught me, and as Dr. Demartini is teaching you now, don't underestimate the power of these laws. Apply them, and the life that you dream about will be yours."

Don't just read this book—follow the Law of Application and put what you read into action.

WORDS OF POWER

I study the laws of the universe, and I apply them.

I know that to know and not to do is not to know.

I am a genius, and I apply my wisdom.

Once I learn a great truth or law, I begin to apply it.

*My amazing life is manifesting because
I am applying wise laws every day.*

I love applying what works; it inspires me.

My Words of Power

_____

_____

_____

_____

_____

_____

_____

_____

My Reflections

How can I use the Law of Application today to fulfill my life's
purpose, dreams, and objectives?

_____

_____

_____

_____

_____

_____

_____

_____

◆◆◆◆◆

Day 44
The Law of Truth

So many common assumptions are just unfounded fantasies! I'm amazed at the number of things people believe that are patently false, such as these:

- I'm supposed to be happy all the time.
- I shouldn't have any sadness.
- I'm supposed to be praised all the time, never criticized.

Many people have these delusions that they're supposed to be in a never-never land of happiness, but by giving this some honest consideration, you can see how foolish they really are. Most folks don't give their assumptions any real scrutiny, though; instead, they just go blithely along with crazy expectations. But *no one* lives a life like that. The truth is that everyone has happiness *and* sadness, and all human beings have niceness and meanness, are pleasant and unpleasant—people have two sides.

If you deny this basic fact, you set yourself up for big crashes and disappointments, as well as depression and feeling like a failure. In fact, I say that the cause of a broken heart is actually a shattered myth or fantasy: Someone expects another person to be a certain way that he or she can't possibly be, and doesn't want him or her to be a complex being. I like to think of these unwise, one-sided expectations in terms of relating to a magnet: Imagine trying to get a one-sided magnet. If you cut it in half, and then in half again, you'll never get just a positive side. There's *always* a positive and a negative side, no matter how many times you divide it.

People are magnetic, too—when you try to get one-sided experiences out of them, they give you two. Likewise, if you try to get just a narrow experience out of life, you'll always be given the whole thing anyway. Going along expecting what isn't possible, getting frustrated when it doesn't happen, and trying to change everything to a one-sided experience will be futile. This is just a way to upset yourself because you can't do the impossible.

When I work with people who are depressed, I find that their disorder is often rooted in the fact that what they think is possible, actually isn't, and they're being hard on themselves because they think that it's their fault. As the Buddha said, the desire for that which isn't attainable is the source of human suffering. People quite often compare *what is* to something that isn't possible, and then put themselves down because they can't match this false idea, blaming themselves because they can't do the impossible. They sometimes chastise others who meet defeat as well.

Dissolve the fantasies and open yourself to the truth, which has two sides. Embrace both: You require support and challenge, positive and negative, and cooperation and conflict to have fulfillment in life. I encourage you to no longer berate yourself or others, because you and they can't live one-sided lives. Begin being grateful that both sides of life enable you to grow in love.

WORDS OF POWER

*The truth is that I have both positive and negative traits,
and both are worth loving.*

I embrace the illusive ups and downs of life, for both teach me to love.

*I embrace support and challenge, praise and criticism,
cooperation and conflict.*

I am grateful for both aspects of my magnetic life.

*Rain and sunshine, cool and warm, storm and calm—
they all help me grow.*

*I love the equal balance of positive and negative traits,
for it gives me freedom.*

MY WORDS OF POWER

_____

_____

_____

_____

_____

_____

_____

_____

MY AMAZING REFLECTIONS

How can I use the Law of Truth today to fulfill my life's
purpose, dreams, and objectives?

_____

_____

_____

_____

_____

_____

_____

◆◆◆◆◆

Day 45
The Law of Speech

Do you know that if you master the art of speaking in front of a group (which is one of the most common fears in the world), great things await you? If you can conquer that dread and proclaim the message lying deep within your heart, you can move to the top 20 percent of the world's achievers. Expressing your ideas with clear and concise diction and articulation moves you to the top 4 percent, and the ability to convey information that moves others can propel you to the top one percent. Those who have the courage to stand up and speak out undeniably have an impact on this planet.

You may wonder, *How do I learn to speak? I'm afraid to get up in front of a group of people because I might be rejected!* I had to overcome this very fear myself, and I was blessed by breaking through it when a gentleman taught me a long time ago that you learn best by doing. He'd tell me, "You learn to play the flute by playing the flute." The same thing is true when it comes to speaking: You learn to speak by simply getting up and presenting your ideas in front of people.

When I started this process, I sometimes stood in front of mirrors and just talked to imaginary audiences. Today, I've finally overcome my fear and can speak to real people, and I do so many times every year. The secret is just getting up and doing it—conquer the fear by taking action.

There's also a very encouraging aspect of the Law of Speaking: You're never in front of an audience you can't handle. As long as you can say, "You know, I don't know the answer to that, but I'll do my best to find out," you're covered.

Cultivate the ability to speak out and share what's deep inside your heart. One of the very earliest speeches I ever made was telling my own story: the tale of how I almost died, how that turned my life around, and how I suddenly discovered my mission for life. I related the way I became dedicated to the study of universal laws as they relate to mind, body, and spirit (particularly in relation to healing). I simply got up and described my experience and my inner feelings, and this was the perfect starting point.

You can begin the same way: Just share your heartfelt story with people you love, and you'll begin to move into the higher percentages of life achievers. *Forbes* magazine once presented a story about people around the world and their levels of wealth. As I was reading it, I realized that my wife and I are right up there with the best of them. I got a tear in my eye, and the thought flashed through my mind: This is due to the power of speaking and the ability to stand up with a message.

Motivational great Zig Ziglar once observed, "You can have everything in life you want if you just help enough other people get what they want." I believe that one of the most powerful ways of inspiring others and helping them get where they want to in life is by sharing a message and a story that inspires them. The power of speech is one of the most effective ways you can accomplish whatever you'd love in life. Every day, make it a point (whether to an invisible audience or a real one) to practice the Law of Speech.

WORDS OF POWER

I share my message and my story from my heart.

I am inspired, and I inspire others.

*I learn to speak by getting up, speaking, and sharing
my story with others.*

I am never in front of an audience I cannot handle.

I am grateful for the gift of speech.

I share my love through my speech.

I practice and perfect my speech.

My voice is the instrument upon which I play the symphony of my life.

MY WORDS OF POWER

_____

_____

_____

_____

_____

_____

_____

_____

MY REFLECTIONS

How can I use the Law of Speech today to fulfill my life's
purpose, dreams, and objectives?

_____

_____

_____

_____

_____

_____

_____

_____

Day 46
The Law of Contingency

W hen you're setting out to accomplish something grand in your life, it's wise to create a thoroughly detailed plan, as well as a backup strategy. Detail your desired outcome, describing exactly how you'd love it to be, and then think of everything that could possibly interfere along the journey so that you can be prepared in advance for any potential challenges that may arise.

Not too long ago, I talked with a gentleman who was involved in planning the construction of a city's monorail. He was asked to help formulate necessary contingency plans for any repercussions or other problems that might occur as it was being built. To do this, he traveled along the proposed train route, going to every different company and individual who lived or worked along the line and asking them what they thought could become a problem or could "go wrong" if the monorail was built near their properties, businesses, or homes. He collected all their concerns, doubts, and ideas; considered them; and included each one in his evolving plan in the form of contingency solutions. When the system was built, he had each possible problem, distraction, and frustration covered so that no matter what happened, the city planners knew what to do.

This man was following the Law of Contingency, understanding that to act is wise and to *react* is foolish. Likewise, when you're laying out your plans, be sure you ask yourself, *What if this happened—or what if that did?* Don't leave anything in doubt, but instead come up with a solution by thinking in advance, *What could be done in this situation?* Then, if these things do occur, there's no problem: You go to plan B or plan C, and you're able to keep your cool.

This process allows you to get ahead by reducing and eliminating the possibilities that could keep you from your dream. By following this law, you're more in command, but without it, you're subject to all types of unexpected actions and reactions. Just as with your finances, there's always going to be something unexpected that comes up in your plans, and if you're not prepared for it, you'll react and become upset.

The Law of Contingency reduces stress and facilitates the fulfillment of your objectives. People who plan ahead get ahead, while those who don't have their fail-safes in place are vulnerable to constant stress and usually fall behind. Follow this law and watch how much more smoothly your dreams come true.

WORDS OF POWER

I am in command. I plan my contingencies in advance.

*I am wise, for I think of all possible obstacles before I begin
and I know what to do when any event arises.*

*I have reduced stress and facilitated my fulfillment because
I plan ahead and solve any potential obstacles in advance.*

*I know how to act instead of <u>react</u> because
I prepare my contingency plans.*

I am way ahead because I planned it that way.

MY WORDS OF POWER

_____

_____

_____

_____

_____

_____

_____

MY REFLECTIONS

How can I use the Law of Contingency today to fulfill my life's purpose, dreams, and objectives?

_____

_____

_____

_____

_____

_____

_____

_____

✦✦✦✦✦

Day 47
The Law of Polarity

In the past, you've probably bought and read at least one book on positive thinking and attempted to be more upbeat in life—and maybe you've purchased a lot more than just that one. Did any of them lead you to feel "up" all the time?

My journey of positive thinking began when I was 18 years old, and I believe I've read most of the available works in that field. But even after perusing so many of them, my negativity still persisted sometimes. I'd try to look on the bright side, but somehow I'd find myself feeling like a failure because I couldn't make it work *all* the time. I'd be downbeat with my wife, kids, or employees; or I'd have an event occur where I'd find myself cursing. Something would happen, I'd get upset, and then I'd beat myself up because of it. *Why am I not able to be continually positive?* I wondered.

For many years, these books had me convinced that I could (and should) be optimistic, helpful, and enthusiastic at all times. But then I finally woke up and realized that it just wasn't humanly possible. I wasn't designed to be perpetually positive, and this was just another fantasy I'd bought into.

One day about 18 years ago, I was in a standing-room-only crowd at a Unity church listening to one of the male leaders of the positive-thinking movement. He stood up on the stage with his wife and said, "Well, you all probably know me as a leader in the field of positive thinking and mental attitude, but I must confess that I'm probably one of the most negative-thinking people you would ever meet." His wife was nodding her head, as if to say, *Oh, is that true! He sure has his negative side.*

That experience awakened me, and I thought, *I can be both positive and negative. I don't have to live as a one-sided being.* This great speaker went on to explain, "I wrote the books on positive thinking to keep me balanced because I'm so negative at times."

Then I began to realize that as I'd come to know all my mentors more personally, I'd seen that they also had their less optimistic aspects. At that point, I set myself free from the false idea that I had to honor only one side of myself. If you find yourself having both sides (being nice and mean, positive and negative, pleasant and unpleasant), be assured that this polarity is perfectly normal and healthy. You're not messed up— you're gifted!

Embrace all of yourself, because you need both sides: Your humbling negativity brings you back into your true center, and your encouraging positivity moves you forward toward your life's dream.

I remember when I first changed my teaching from all-positive thinking to a balanced and openhearted philosophy: 75 people walked out of the room saying, "We don't want to hear that!" I was frightened and almost unwilling to keep sharing this law, because I was afraid of their reaction, but today I realize that this balance is the truth. Now I'm not worried about anyone walking out. They stay because they realize a new possibility in life: They don't have to be someone they aren't; they can be who they are with a balance of positive and negative thinking.

You can live this truth, too, so apply the Law of Polarity, embracing both sides of yourself and both sides of others. You're magnificent!

WORDS OF POWER

I thank God for my balance of positive and negative traits,
for both are centered in love.

I am a perfect balance of equally positive and negative traits,
and I embrace myself.

The universe has a perfect balance of positive and negative,
and I am one with the universe.

My heart opens as I see the benefits of my positive and negative sides.

I embrace my light and my shadow sides, for both help me love.
I am free to be who I am and to love myself as I am,
and I love others as they are.

MY WORDS OF POWER

_____

_____

_____

_____

_____

_____

_____

MY REFLECTIONS

How can I use the Law of Polarity today to fulfill my life's
purpose, dreams, and objectives?

_____

_____

_____

_____

_____

_____

_____

Day 48
The Law of Reasonable Expectations

The interesting truth is that most of the time you probably put totally *unrealistic* expectations on yourself (and others). For example, you might expect everyone to be nice 24 hours a day, but human nature is to be both nice and mean. Or you might count on being totally successful and never failing, but at least half the time you *won't* succeed. (Keep in mind that Babe Ruth hit the most home runs, but he also had the most strikeouts!)

If you look carefully, you'll realize that you probably run around with many illusory fantasies about what you're supposed to be like or do. The truth is, you're a "both-sided" being, as I explained in earlier parts of this book, and the Law of Reasonable Expectation is the ability to allow yourself to have this quality.

Someone once told me, "Well, John, you're somebody who walks your talk. That's why you're successful." Well, if I'm really honest and humble, I realize that I *don't* always "walk my talk"—in fact, sometimes I just "limp my life."

Like most teachers, I find that what I share the most emphatically is often what I most need to learn. I realize that if I had the expectation that I was supposed to be this person who was only upbeat, I'd be beating myself up every day because I couldn't live up to that unreasonable expectation. When I tried to be "Mr. Optimist" all the time and didn't allow myself the down side occasionally (as I described earlier), I was putting myself down because I wasn't allowing myself the healthy skepticism or pessimism required for leading a centered and balanced life.

I believe that the reason some people have diseases is that they have unrealistic expectations about others and themselves. They continue to have misleading dreams about the way they expect life to be, and the world doesn't fit in to their illusions.

The Law of Reasonable Expectations means that you attempt to walk your talk, but you also allow yourself to falter at times. It also means that you can set high expectations for yourself—if they can be realized.

Years ago I was listening to a great motivational speaker. After his talk, I walked up to him and asked, "How do I become an international professional speaker?"

"Start telling people you are," he answered.

I exclaimed, "But I'm not!"

"Tell people you are. Start preempting it," he urged, and I couldn't help arguing again, "But that's not true!"

"So," he repeated, "start telling people it is, until it *becomes* true."

I let him know that this struck me as a kind of lie, and he just said, "Welcome to the reality of prophecy—of creating things!"

At first, I judged his advice harshly—but I started doing it inwardly anyway. I didn't tell anyone else because I was afraid of their reaction, so I began by saying *I'm an international professional speaker* to myself.

Then about two weeks later, someone asked me, "What do you do for a living?" and I replied, "I'm an international professional speaker." I was amazed that shortly after this incident, I was asked to give my first international professional speech, and at that point I understood that I needed to allow myself to create my outcomes. I began by distorting my present reality in order to build my future reality.

It seemed weird. I realized that when I didn't always walk my talk—and when I sometimes "limped my life"—my realistic expectations started to materialize, rather than any far-fetched visions I had. I'd awakened my ability to allow myself to be all that I dreamed of being, and it worked.

To begin this process, scan your current life and think of all the unrealistic expectations that you have that are truly impossible—actions that you may be expecting of yourself that are one-sided. Now reset them by changing them into reasonable ones, and then go and make them possible.

True possibility thinking isn't fantasy; it's being reality based and acting according to those principles. The Law of Reasonable Expectations is yours for the taking.

I promise you, however, that no matter what you're doing, you're on track. You're being guided and directed through feedback, so that whatever you've done has served. Just know that you're already on your way, and be reasonable with yourself. Permit the true expectation of something doable, and you'll change your life as you watch how your past limping along the path becomes your future walking tall.

WORDS OF POWER

*My dreams are reasonable, and every day I make and
take another step toward their fulfillment.*

*I have a balanced expectation of myself,
and that is why I am productive.*

I limp my life until I walk my talk, and then I run and soar!

Every day I do something to make my dreams more real.

I set reasonable, balanced, and livable objectives.

My path to true fulfillment has a balance of successes and failures.

MY WORDS OF POWER

MY REFLECTIONS

How can I use the Law of Reasonable Expectations today to fulfill
my life's purpose, dreams, and objectives?

_____

_____

_____

_____

_____

_____

_____

_____

Day 49
The Law of Detail

As I've traveled and taught around the world, I've often observed my students writing down their dreams and goals in very general, unspecified ways. They sometimes make such general statements as "I'd love to have more money." Yet ill-defined wishes such as these seldom help them reach their goals because the words are too vague. If you'd love to accomplish something in your life, it pays to get specific about the nitty-gritty of your vision. Start with the big picture, and then visualize and write down every detail if you truly desire to manifest such dreams.

For example, let's imagine that I wanted to build a tall building and I have 200 workers at my disposal. I'd tell them, "All right—go build this tall building over there!"

Naturally, they'd ask me, "What exactly do you want us to do?"

"I want a 70-story building," might be my reply, but still needing more information, they'd come back with another question: "Um, do you have the plans?"

Insisting, "No, I don't have any plans. Just go build a 70-story building," wouldn't help, and by now they'd be getting a little perturbed. "We need to have some details! How tall do you want it?"

Saying, "I want it 70 stories, ten feet per story," would be a little more helpful, and they might answer, "Okay, now we're getting somewhere!" but the finer points would still have to be worked out: "What's the floor plan? What does it look like? What's the shape?" In other words, they couldn't construct anything until they had thorough information—and neither can you build your dreams until you hammer out the details.

When I encourage my students to write down their goals, I hover over them and push them to include more information. When they say that they want a car, I ask, "What color is the interior? How fast is it going to go? What does it look like? What brand is it?" The more they know, the more masterful their creation will be.

When I'd love to create or accomplish something, and I truly honor that dream, I'll take the time to visualize and plan out the details. For example, when I had my chiropractic practice, I'd just sit in my office sometimes, close my eyes, and imagine what patient I'd love to see that day. What would they be doing, and what would I be saying? How would I actually manage them? What would I be doing to get referrals of new patients? I'd go through every detail in my mind, and then it showed up in my life.

The one who's able to conquer the details is a master architect, and you're here to build not just a skyscraper, but a "lifescraper." You're here to accomplish something big! It takes no more effort to make something enormous than something small. After all, no one gets up in the morning and says, "Oh, I wish I could be, do, and have nothing," so go for something impressive in life, and remember the details! The Law of Detail is the secret of making your life a masterpiece.

WORDS OF POWER

Every day I refine the details of my dream.

*I am a master architect, for I see the details and
I use them to build my dreams.*

I am a master who focuses on ever-finer detail.

I visualize my dreams in fine detail, and they show up in my life.

*I leave as little as possible to chance and plan
my details out before someone else does.*

*The inspiring details lying within my mind and heart are
what distinguish me from others.*

MY WORDS OF POWER

_____

_____

_____

_____

_____

_____

_____

_____

MY REFLECTIONS

How can I use the Law of Detail today to fulfill my life's
purpose, dreams, and objectives?

_____

_____

_____

_____

_____

_____

_____

_____

✦✦✦✦✦

167

Week
EIGHT

Day 50
The Law of Marketing

This principle is one that you might not see in most marketing texts, but it's something you'll observe if you look around carefully. Imagine what would happen if you went to work thinking, *Oh, crud! I have to go to work today.* You'd feel awful. If you're in this mood, you're exhaling desperation more than inhaling inspiration—you're *de*-spired rather than *in*-spired—and if you start your day in this way, whatever type of work you're in will actually tend to go downward.

This form of energy says to the world, "I'm overwhelmed! I don't really love doing what I'm doing today, and I don't want to be here." Your heart isn't into your business at the moment, and as a result, your customers probably won't be as attracted to you or your company. If you had a certain number of clients scheduled, you'll probably reduce them by half throughout the day (or your traffic will at least go down); cancellations may become likely, and new opportunities may lessen. Your inner energy and intention reverses any outward marketing efforts.

On the other hand, suppose you think, *I want to go to work today!* You'll have what I call a "want to" day: "Have to" leads to break down and "want to" leads to break even. Even if you're not necessarily inspired, you *want to* go to work, make a living, and go out and market yourself. In this case, whatever number of clients you had scheduled for that day will be about the same as the results you achieve: You'll break even.

Now imagine that you go to work telling yourself, *Wow—I love it!* You hear yourself throughout the day saying: *I love it! I love it! I love it! This is inspiring! Wow! Incredible! So powerful! So fulfilling! I love it!* Your energy is up, and in this case, instead of breaking down or breaking even, you break *through.* Now you break records, and rather than your scheduled number of customers (or half that amount), you get two or three times the clients for that day. You seem to explode and attract opportunities.

This is a phenomenon that I call the "Cosmic Marketing System." If you're in the "have to" mode, you shut off this power; at the "want to" level, you turn it on; and at the "love to" level, you shoot it through the roof.

People ask me how I developed my marketing strategy throughout the world, and I tell them the truth: "Just doing what I love, and loving what I do." Here are your affirmations to achieve the same thing: *I do what I love. I love what I do. I love going to work. My work is my play, and my play is my work. My avocation is my vocation, and my vocation is my avocation. I love it!*

Say those sentences every day . . . I don't mean that you should get elated or infatuated with your work—instead, *love it.* This means that you embrace both sides of whatever happens each day with equanimity and poise, knowing that everything serves and inspires as a form of feedback toward your desired objective. I take the support, the challenges, the positives, and the negatives equally because I know that I grow from both sides.

Attaining this state of mind where you can truly be inspired by your work and enthused to do it is called *self-actualization,* and the Law of Marketing will take you there. I guarantee that it will help you grow professionally, and you'll break through.

WORDS OF POWER

I do what I love! I love what I do!
I am inspired by going to work.
I love serving my clients, and my work is fulfilling and inspiring.
My state of inspiration draws new clients to me like a magnet.
I love my work no matter what happens, because
I know that it is leading me to self-mastery.

I put the Cosmic Marketing System to work for me
because I love what I do!
I love going to work! My work is my play. My vocation is my vacation.

MY WORDS OF POWER

_____

_____

_____

_____

_____

_____

_____

_____

MY REFLECTIONS

How can I use the Law of Marketing today to fulfill my life's
purpose, dreams, and objectives?

_____

_____

_____

_____

_____

_____

_____

_____

✦✦✦✦✦

Day 51
The Law of Study

You may be thinking that a Law of Study sounds pretty uninspiring. I can just hear you saying, "I finished school years ago. I don't want to go back and crack the books." But you probably also realize that when you finished your formal education, the practical, real-life learning began, and now you get to apply everything you absorb.

What area(s) of life do you intend to learn about and master? Expertise of any kind requires effort, even if it's not the same kind of all-night cram sessions you may have experienced when you were younger. Did you know that if you studied intensively for just about any subject three hours a day, you could become an expert in relatively short order—potentially in just a few years? Here are some facts to consider:

- It's been shown that if people study even 30 minutes a day, in seven years they can be at the leading edge of their area of interest.

- If they study an hour a day, in around four to five years they can achieve the same results.

- Two hours of work each day can lead to the same goal in about two and a half to three years.

- Studying three hours a day means that in two years or less they can be at the forefront of their field.

I used this idea of concentrated learning many years ago, and I followed this time-line principle for a number of subjects. First, I set out to make a list of all the "-ologies," all the different disciplines that I wanted to master in my life. I wrote them down and investigated what reading or other requirements it would take to receive a master's or doctoral degree in each field. I came to realize that the average person who gets a doctorate reads 75 to 80 books in that particular area of expertise, and I figured I could do that in many subjects.

Even though they say today that you should specialize, I believe that some of the greatest people in history had general knowledge in many different areas. Some of the most inspired geniuses (such as Leonardo da Vinci and Hildegard of Bingen) excelled in many areas, so, using them as my examples, I set out to understand and master many fields.

Among many other subjects I've applied myself to (including acquiring the skill of speed-reading), years ago I wanted to study dentistry. I went to the University of Texas dental school and asked, "What are the curricula and texts that I would normally study to get my doctorate degree here?" The dean of admissions directed me to the book requirements, and I then devoured every necessary text. Less than two years later, I had the opportunity to lecture at a number of dental conferences as a specialist in that field. I proved to myself that if I studied something diligently for a few hours a day, I could be a master and reach the leading edge of knowledge.

Some people say that this isn't possible, but I'm giving you the key to making it happen: If you study every day, even for a few minutes, it may take you longer than completing a conventional academic program, but you'll eventually reach the upper echelons. After most people receive their degrees, they reduce the amount of their study time and review only old literature and a few journals. But believe me: You can study, and you can be a master—and just a few hours a day can make the difference. Even a few *minutes* a day can eventually help make you an expert. Decide what you'd love to master and follow the Law of Study; become a diligent lifetime student.

Words of Power

I love studying, and I am mastering a number of fields.
I study daily.
I am a persevering student of life.
Daily I study truth. Daily I share my wisdom.
I love to study what most inspires me.
My study fuels my inspiration. My inspiration fuels my study.
I am a master reader: Whatever I read, I retain.

My Words of Power

_____

_____

_____

_____

_____

_____

_____

_____

MY REFLECTIONS

How can I use the Law of Study today to fulfill my life's
purpose, dreams, and objectives?

_____

_____

_____

_____

_____

_____

_____

✦✦✦✦✦

Day 52
The Law of Integration

When people experience love and appreciation, their brains and hearts become energetically integrated as their brain and heart waves synchronize. In that state, the power of human intent is optimal, and you have the ability to create! When you have love in your heart and poise in your mind, you also have an integration of your left and right brain, as they become aligned, too. Your heart's intuition and your brain's reason become one, congruent and centered. You have a power that can't be shaken or rocked, for with love, appreciation, and integration, you're stable and adaptable in your environment, like a martial artist who's trained to remain centered but who goes with the flow of circumstances. Since you're steadfast in your intent, it shows in your outcomes: No matter what the obstacles, you accomplish your objectives.

Love and appreciation are the most masterful states of being. Years ago I asked, "What's the underlying secret for attaining this condition?" I came to realize that with a balanced perspective, you don't get sidetracked, vacillate, or emotionalize. Instead, you experience inspiration and become centered. The secret of the Law of Integration is that you stay focused on your mission and purpose, and remain present and inspired about your life and what you do. Gratitude allows you to appreciate what you have, and you get more when you're grateful.

When you become congruently integrated, you have wellness, but when you become disintegrated, you breed illness. Your body's signs and symptoms are attempting to give you feedback to get you to break your illusions and lack of gratitude, and to awaken you to the truth, which will bring you to a state of appreciation and love.

Fear and guilt cause you to fracture yourself, but you become integrated into one being when you have love and appreciation. The latter are your most powerful states, for they cause your feelings to attract people, magnetizing opportunities. The Law of Integration is a magnificent key to an amazing and fulfilling life. Apply it, be grateful, and love your life!

WORDS OF POWER

My heart and mind become integrated as I grow in love and gratitude.

Love and appreciation bring my mind and heart together.
I am my true self.

I am centered in love and appreciation. I am powerfully integrated.

In love and appreciation, my intent is optimal.
I have power to do what I love.

My creativity expands as my mind and heart
become one in love and gratitude.

My right and left brain work together in unison
when I exist in love and gratitude.

My heart's intuition and my mind's reason
become one in love and gratitude.

My heart and my mind become one in love and appreciation.

MY WORDS OF POWER

_____

_____

_____

_____

_____

_____

_____

MY REFLECTIONS

How can I use the Law of Integration today to fulfill my life's purpose, dreams, and objectives?

_____

_____

_____

_____

_____

_____

_____

Day 53
The Law of Quality

Every single person is at some stage or level of development. I don't know of anyone who gets up in the morning and says, "I wish I could be less, do less, have less in life, and be more impoverished. I wish I could drive a worse-looking car—a rusted, beat-up model that barely runs and has no air conditioning!" No one I know can honestly say they'd love that.

In all probability, most people wake up in the morning thinking (in their own way), *I want to expand myself and broaden my horizons. I'd love to have a more meaningful and loving relationship, a fine car, and a beautiful home. It would be wonderful to become even more aware.*

You see, most people would love to grow.

To evolve to the next step or plateau, it's wise to be willing to raise the bar on the scale of quality. For instance, I remember buying a $100 suit when I was working at J. C. Penney. (It was reversible as well, so you could wear it two ways.) I thought that was a pretty amazing deal. Now I realize that that was my first step on the scale of quality. Next I bought a $200 suit, and since then I've graduated into more expensive, higher-quality clothing as I've been able to afford and appreciate it. The finer pieces look nicer and last longer, and I feel better when I wear them, which means that I act differently. I've learned that quality makes a difference.

If you go to an inexpensive restaurant that gives you a plastic spoon and plate, you'll have a different level of respect for the art of creating and eating food than you would in a five-star, fine-dining facility where quality presentation is a must. You're designed to grow, and to expand and prosper, so you naturally desire to keep pushing yourself to higher levels.

Imagine walking past a street display and seeing some cheap art and then going to a fine museum where you can view a masterpiece. Now put this in relation to your daily existence: If you surround yourself with quality, you learn to express quality. Make it your goal to say, "Today I'm going to expand myself just a little further." I encourage you, no matter what your lifestyle, to attempt to increase it by at least 10 percent every year. Beat out inflation and grow. If you don't, you're stagnating, and once you account for inflation, that means that you're actually going backward.

So take a step forward and make it a goal to say, "I'd love to go from one quality of clothing to the next, and even to the level beyond that. I want this degree of excellence in my car and home. I increase my caliber in relationships and every area of life that's important to me." Step up! There's nothing inherently wrong with higher quality—you're investing in people who are masters of their art, rather than in those who don't respect themselves and just put something quick out onto the market. Invest in quality, and you honor yourself and the universe. You're worth it.

Say to yourself each day: *My quality grows with every day that I live: the quality of what I eat, the quality of the clothes I wear, the quality of where I live and where I travel, the quality of my companions, and the quality of my relationships. The quality of my own integrity and of the understanding of my true self is magnified. The quality of everything I do is upgraded.* As a result, you'll live a quality life.

As long as you accept less than what you dream about, you'll keep receiving it; and as long as you accept less than what you'd love, you'll keep experiencing that. Ask yourself—and push yourself—to go beyond. When you decide to stay in a nicer place and pay a little bit more, you'll become accustomed to it, and you'll find that you'll begin to attract a new set of friends, great opportunities, and fresh ways of doing things. Quality works!

Right by the phone in my office I have a placard that reminds me: "Quality first!" Why spend your precious time and life on anything less? The process of increasing excellence makes a huge difference in your daily outcomes. Years ago I often gave my seminars for nothing, and they never seemed to get off the ground. Nobody valued them. Later I presented the same material for *something:* I made attendees compensate me. Now these evolved workshops attract people from all over and are held across the globe. People receive what they pay for, so if you'd love to experience an amazing life, be willing to pay for it—and *be* paid for it. Go for the Law of Quality.

WORDS OF POWER

Quality first!
The quality of my life grows with every day of my life.
Every day in every way I increase the quality of my lifestyle.
I provide quality service for a quality price and live an amazing life.
The quality of everything I do is upgraded daily.
Quality works!

MY WORDS OF POWER

_____

_____

_____

_____

_____

_____

_____

MY REFLECTIONS

How can I use the Law of Quality today to fulfill my life's
purpose, dreams, and objectives?

_____

_____

_____

_____

_____

_____

_____

_____

Day 54
The Law of Expression and Repression

If you dig deep into your psychological and emotional makeup, you'll discover two components: The first is the one where you feel you're better or greater than you truly are, where you exaggerate your accomplishments by thinking you're "bigger than." This is your extroverted self that thinks, *I can do it. I'm everything! I'm better!*

The second part is the one where you feel you're worse or less than you truly are, where you minimize yourself, thinking you're "smaller than." This is your introverted self, where you think, *I can't do it. I'm nothing! I'm worse!*

One part of you builds up, and another tears down; and when these two aspects are realized at the same time, the central you is awakened. This is your true and transformative self. You have a dual personality revolving around a truly centered you, and when you emotionally elevate or depress your perception of yourself, you express and repress these personalities. When you integrate and center yourself, you become empowered and truly love.

Yet if you vacillate between these two, expressing one while repressing the other, you can feel like Dr. Jekyll and Mr. Hyde. Publicly you may be very optimistic, but you're privately pessimistic—nice during the day, mean at night; extremely extroverted, very introverted! Actually, both occur at the same time, but as you choose to own (express) and disown (repress) each of these parts, you can feel them oscillate. One woman told me, "During the day, I'm 'Miss Optimist,' a total extrovert. But when I get home, I just shut the telephone off and hide out. I become a hermit."

You don't have to live at the two extremes. As I discussed earlier, when you're grateful and integrated, your heart opens in love, and these components of your personality come together as the expressed and repressed join. Suddenly you're your true self, made up of these two sides.

Apply this to the art of communication: Imagine going on a date when you're in a highly self-righteous mode, and you're seeing someone who has a "self-wrongeous" attitude. Although you may initially assume that you're both at the same level, the other person is actually at their low point, while you're at your high point. In this scenario, you may minimize him or her, and they may exaggerate you. He or she will start out on your date rather infatuated, and you'll be rather blah; or you may try to rescue this person. Since you're both wearing masks, the relationship has an unstable beginning.

True love requires an open heart, which can't exist when you're trying to hide one part of yourself by wearing another aspect as a disguise. Yet when you're able to honor and exhibit all of yourself—the true you—you can be balanced and open your heart.

When your feelings are centered, you experience love. When they're lopsided, however, you have extreme emotions that can reveal distortions, lies, and exaggerations about your life. Your greatest potential and magnitude of opportunity occurs when you're focused. Through the Law of Expression and Regression, each behavior teaches you to hone yourself—they represent positive and negative feedback to help you become who you truly are.

WORDS OF POWER

Thank you, universe, for the positive and negative feedback you give me, which centers me in love.

My heart opens in love as I embrace my two sides.

No matter what I have done or not done, I am worthy of love.

My true self is balanced and magnificent.

When I am up, I look for the downs.
When I am down, I look for the ups.

My exaggerations and minimizations dissolve when I am grateful.
Love is equilibrium between expression and repression.

MY WORDS OF POWER

_____

_____

_____

_____

_____

_____

_____

MY REFLECTIONS

How can I use the Law of Expression and Repression today to
fulfill my life's purpose, dreams, and objectives?

_____

_____

_____

_____

_____

_____

_____

✦ ✦ ✦ ✦ ✦

Day 55
The Law of Order

When I was 18 years old, I sat in the center of my room at my parents' home and read a book by Gottfried Wilhelm Leibniz called *Discourse on Metaphysics.* On the very first page of this text was an idea that inspired me so much it brought tears to my eyes: Leibniz had uncovered the great principles of divine order, divine perfection, and divine magnificence in the universe. I didn't understand at first why that touched me so deeply, but I began a quest at that time to discover why this had such an impact on me, and I somehow inwardly sensed that there truly was an underlying order in the world—that is, that life is purposeful.

You probably go along observing events and thinking, *That's bad!* or *That's good!* Yet a week, a month, or a few years later, you could look back at the so-called bad event and see that it wasn't so horrible after all. You'd see how it served you, although at the moment you thought it was unbelievably difficult. Looking back, you might think, *Thank God that occurred!* And that event you thought was so terrific? Perhaps you were going to acquire a new house or make some other major purchase, but now you see the responsibilities and consequences, such as new taxes, the cost of upkeep, and a lot of additional work. Your wonderful thing has some drawbacks, and those "terrifics" now have some "terribles" attached to them.

In other words, time and nature attempt to teach you to find the balance in life, which is the hidden divine order that Leibniz described so eloquently. He said that few individuals grasp this truth, and that the masters of life are the ones who see this in the universe. The majority continue ticktocking along, saying, "Oh, this is awful!" and "Oh, this is great!" They act like passive victims, rather than victors who know life's inherent beauty.

Why wait for days, weeks, or months to discover that all things exist in order? Why not achieve this wisdom of the ages without the aging process? The moment that you label an event as "dreadful," look for the blessing, and the moment you think an event is wonderful, look for its downside. Keeping your perceptions in balance is what I call "collapsing the illusion" and opening your heart to the truth, which is that love is everywhere and in everything.

Rather than live in "terrible" or "terrific," why not dwell in the center? The truth—the Law of Order—is that inside every experience (which is a neutral event) lies the opportunity for the balance of opposites. No matter how you perceive anything, always look for the other side; you'll find the order, and your life will become even more amazing.

WORDS OF POWER

There is nothing but love. All else is illusion.

Every experience is the opportunity to see the balance of opposites.

I look until I see the perfectly balanced perspective in gratitude.

I look for the downs in the "terrifics," the ups in the "terribles."
Everything leads to love.

My heart opens in love as I see the hidden order in life.

I see the light of love in all things.

I see life's beauty as I see life's balance.

MY WORDS OF POWER

_____

_____

_____

_____

_____

_____

_____

_____

MY REFLECTIONS

How can I use the Law of Order today to fulfill my life's
purpose, dreams, and objectives?

_____

_____

_____

_____

_____

_____

_____

Day 56
The Law of Adaptability

If you're unable to adapt to your environment, you can't survive—so said Dr. Hans Selye, an endocrinologist who studied stress all his adult life. The man whom many called "the Einstein of medicine" emphasized how essential it is to be flexible and pliant.

It was recently discovered that the human brain is highly changeable, able to constantly remodel itself—this means that every time you think new thoughts or have new feelings, your brain remolds itself, forming new neural pathways and connections. This adaptability is essential to your development as an individual and to human evolution, so when you set goals, don't be so rigid with your plans that you attempt to force things in order to accomplish them. The secret to mastering your mind is to remain adaptable to newly emerging events and insights as you pursue your dreams.

The Law of Adaptability depends upon your willingness to keep refining, defining, and acclimatizing again and again to the events and situations you experience in life. This isn't to be confused with procrastination or wavering on your goals; instead, the challenge here is to flex your plans and dreams, meaning that you're not so rigid and stuck in your own ways that you're unable to take advantage of new opportunities that come along.

For example, I once dreamed of building a magnificent clinic. I'd envisioned it as a multistory, broad-based building. About three months into working on the project, another opportunity emerged: An office was available, which wasn't exactly what I had in mind (but was very similar to it), yet the price and location were irresistible. Although it wasn't precisely what I'd imagined at the time, it was actually even more suit-able, and by not locking myself rigidly into the exact form of my ideas for growth, I was able to adapt and get one step closer to my dream.

Be adaptable, keep your eyes open, and don't get so narrowly focused that you can't see even greater possibilities ahead. Just as your body doesn't function well if it's too rigid, so it is with your mind and your dreams. Allow yourself the flexibility to continuously evolve and follow the Law of Adaptability.

WORDS OF POWER

I am adaptable. New events, insights,
and refinements enable me to fulfill my purpose.

I am grateful for the opportunity to
refine my goals and dreams for life.

I keep my eyes open for new possibilities.

As all living things change, I am evolving in the life I love.

I am flexible in my persistence and persistent in my flexibility.

Because of my adaptability, I am becoming more refined daily.

MY WORDS OF POWER

_____

_____

_____

_____

_____

_____

_____

My Reflections

How can I use the Law of Adaptability today to fulfill my life's
purpose, dreams, and objectives?

❖❖❖❖❖

Week
NINE

Day 57
The Law of Condemnation

Working with thousands of individuals around the world, I've observed that whatever people condemn, they actually tend to create, draw to them, or become. In other words, if there are parts of yourself you disown, you're likely to attract these qualities in others.

For instance, if you can't stand the way someone eats, the way they look, or some other habit of theirs (whatever it may be), stop and take a look in the mirror. Ask yourself, *Where do I see in _myself_ the things I can't stand in them? Where do _I_ have this trait of theirs, and who sees it in me in some way?* If you humble yourself rather than judging others and becoming self-righteous, not only is there a higher probability of a shift in *their* behavior, but you'll learn to know and love them and *yourself* as well. When you're humble, you tend to get more assistance than resistance.

If you look closely enough, perhaps you'll see yourself as others do. It's almost certain that you're doing these same troublesome things in some form or other. I've heard it said that the seer, the seeing, and the seen are the same. That is, you can only pick out what and how you are, so whatever you find in others is a reflection of yourself. Remember the biblical caution: It's wise to pluck the beam out of your own eye before you try to take a speck from another's.

Realize that condemnation just breeds more disgust over the same situation within yourself. One young lady who came to my seminar said, "I'd never do this in my life. Never!" However, about six months later, she confessed, "I can't believe I said that. Three of the things that I swore I'd never do have now come into my life."

Instead of belittling others, understand that everything has a time and a place, and nothing's here to be put down, just understood. Open your heart and love: Rather than continually trying to force others to change, appreciate them for who they are, for everyone and everything has lessons to teach. The Law of Condemnation is a constant reminder to appreciate what you have and the people who share your life.

WORDS OF POWER

I look within myself for the things that I condemn in others.
What I see is me.
Everything serves and teaches me. I look until I see blessings.
I have all traits, so I embrace in myself what I see in others.
I find the blessings in every trait and event.
When I am humble, I truly love others, and myself, as well.
Humility is the courage of the truth.

MY WORDS OF POWER

_____

_____

_____

_____

_____

_____

_____

_____

_____

My Reflections

How can I use the Law of Condemnation today to fulfill my life's purpose, dreams, and objectives?

_____

_____

_____

_____

_____

_____

_____

Day 58
The Law of Dominant Thought

You may have heard the axiom "What you think about, you bring about." How true this is! You attract into your life those things that are related to what you send out in the form of your thoughts. Your innermost dominant thought becomes your outermost tangible reality. Therefore, it's wise to examine your thinking process. You see, you're either ruled by your inspirations or by one of two "desperations": The first is something with which you're infatuated; the second is something that you resent.

For example, imagine that you're walking down the street and see something you really admire. You think that there are more positives than negatives in this object, and it distracts you and takes up space and time in your mind. You suddenly find your thinking dominated by it, and perhaps you can think of nothing else. You're now being ruled by infatuation—it's acting as a kind of drug being released in your brain.

On the other hand, you may be driving down the street when someone cuts you off or runs into you. You resent that event and see more negatives than positives. You cannot quit thinking about it, and suddenly *that* takes over your mind. In other words, anything you're *extremely* emotional about—or which you become infatuated with or resentful toward—controls you.

However, if you were to take those infatuations and resentments and bring them back into equilibrium until you're centered, then you could let that which truly inspires you dominate your thoughts. You see, you're either run by the outer world and therefore attract events into your life because of your outer circumstances and misperceptions, or you're ruled by your inner world, resonating with your inspirations.

I like to think of this from a theological perspective: You're either controlled by your senses or your soul. If your soul's in charge, then the things you love in life dominate your thoughts and you attract them into your life. Otherwise, you're governed by your senses, and the world around you calls the shots.

Again, your innermost dominant thought becomes your outermost tangible reality. You can choose either to emotionalize your life and become a victim, or you can be inspired and become a victor. You control this, so if you don't take the time to put into your thinking how you'd love your life to be, then you're vulnerable to the outer sensory world. I recommend that you stop and reflect on the following: *What would I truly love to dominate my thoughts? What would I truly love to have as the center of my life?* Every day that you zero in on what you love gives you another opportunity to attract and create that.

Imagine if you spent 24 hours reining in your random ideas and instead focused on how you'd love your life to be. The Law of Dominant Thought will help you master your life.

WORDS OF POWER

My innermost dominant thought becomes my outermost tangible reality.
I think of what I would love to be, do, and have in ever-finer detail.
I look to see what I am thinking, for I know it will manifest!
I focus on exactly how I would love my life to be.
I listen to my soul. My thoughts on what I would love in life dominate.
*I resonate with my inspirations and let go of my
infatuations and resentments.*
I choose to be inspired in my life! I am a victor, not a victim.

MY WORDS OF POWER

_____

_____

_____

_____

_____

_____

_____

_____

MY REFLECTIONS

How can I use the Law of Dominant Thought today to fulfill my life's purpose, dreams, and objectives?

_____

_____

_____

_____

_____

_____

_____

Day 59
The Law of Space and Time

Imagine that you're going to work and you don't have a tightly booked schedule. Do you know what will happen once you arrive? The mail will distract you, colleagues and friends will call, and salespeople will show up—all kinds of things seem to come and fill the day. Whatever space and time you have in your life will become filled with low priorities if you don't fill it with higher ones. An old Latin proverb cautions us that nature abhors a vacuum. Today, it's obvious that if you don't fill your hours with what you love, the world will fill them with the things you don't care for.

The secret of using this law effectively is to be certain that every minute of your day is devoted to things you love. When I was in my healing practice years ago, I learned that anytime I wasn't working with patients, I'd better come up with a list of high-priority things to do—I could then use every bit of my workday to build my practice or serve more people. If for some reason I wasn't directly serving a patient for a moment, my list reminded me to write a thank-you letter, give someone a birthday call, practice some sort of communication skill, or read some new clinical information. Since every minute of my day was filled with high-priority actions, my productivity soared.

Don't allow yourself idle time, or you'll find it overrun with low-priority actions. Instead, make your own agenda and take command of your space and time—after all, either it rules you, or you rule it. The secret is to make sure that you, from your heart, plan into your schedule what you'd love to receive. This may mean leaving in time for rest or meditation, but the key is *scheduling* it. Know in advance what you intend, start the day as you've planned, and then see whether you can live exactly as you've imagined.

When you go through your life with an agenda and with your tasks prioritized, you'll cluster and condense your activities to rule your space and time. Otherwise, you'll become distracted by the vagaries of life and won't know where you're going. Follow the Law of Space and Time to take command of your daily destiny.

WORDS OF POWER

I fill my day with high-priority actions.

I plan into my day what I would love to get out of it.

I transform my "idle" time into planned-activity time and create the life I love.

My time is precious. I use it for what I would love most.

I love to fill my space and time with things I love.

I know where I am going, and I plan and use my time wisely.

I am grateful for each minute, and I use each one for the things I love.

MY WORDS OF POWER

_____

_____

_____

_____

_____

_____

_____

MY REFLECTIONS

How can I use the Law of Space and Time today to fulfill my life's purpose, dreams, and objectives?

_____

_____

_____

_____

_____

_____

_____

_____

Day 60
The Law of Prayer

When most people think of prayer, they think of asking for help from a Higher Source to aid them in the traumas, tragedies, or anxious circumstances of their lives. Other people, when they become excited with the way things seem to be, say, "Oh, thank you! Thank you, God! Thank you, universe! Thank you!" Their prayer is one of elation. Most individuals pray when they're really sad or really happy, really down or really up.

The secret of the most powerful prayer is to call on God not when you're ecstatic or depressed, but when you're poised, centered in your heart, and grateful. You're in God's presence then, not asking God to change this situation or fix that person, but grateful for all that is, as it is. This is the highest of prayers, which acknowledges the order of the universe rather than denying it. This contrasts with sitting before the order of the universe and thinking, *Oh, I wish it would change and match what I imagine would support me.*

The truest of prayers has reverence for the universal perfection. Now *there's* something to be grateful for! The highest and most powerful worship offers gratitude and asks nothing as it expresses thankfulness for what is, as it is. It has appreciation for every day, what you've been given, the opportunities to share and serve, all the people who come into your life, and all your experiences.

A great power is unleashed when you follow the Law of Prayer and are willing to see this universal magnificence with eyes of gratitude and say thank you. Don't spend your time waiting until you're down, and don't wait until you're elated. On a daily basis, be centered, focused, and in love, through this highest of prayers. This amazing power is truly an act of love and grace.

WORDS OF POWER

I am centered and focused in love through the prayer of gratitude.
I am grateful for all that is, as it is.
I am grateful for the divine order, the divine perfection,
and the divine magnificence of the universe.
I see how everything is in order!
Daily, I sit in silence and pray with a heart of gratitude.

MY WORDS OF POWER

_____

_____

_____

_____

_____

_____

_____

_____

MY REFLECTIONS

How can I use the Law of Prayer today to fulfill my life's
purpose, dreams, and objectives?

_____

_____

_____

_____

_____

_____

_____

The Law of Finale

When setting goals and thinking of what you'd truly love in life, you may have heard of the "last is first" principle. I call it the Law of Finale. In other words, when you're making plans in your life, the first principle is to start with the final end product. Management expert Stephen Covey says it in this way: "Begin with the end in mind." I say that you should see the final outcome of what you imagine, and start from there.

I learned this from an architect who designs many of the world's sky-scrapers. He begins his process by creating a model of how he'd love his building to look. He then imagines every detail, working his way back to these thoughts: *What would I love to do here? What goes there? How does this look?* He continues until he gets to the first thing he'd love to do—so he starts with the last and finds his way to the beginning.

I use this principle whenever I plan. For example, when I'm writing a book, I precisely imagine the final product that I'd love to see, and then I ask myself about the different pieces—the theme, the title, the four car-dinal messages, and then three sub-messages for each one. Next, I bring it down into ever-finer detail, asking myself, *What paragraphs, what sentences, and finally, what words would I love to use?* I work my way back from the final product all the way down to the smallest detail that I can act on today.

Begin with the outcome you hold in your heart and trace your way to daily action steps. If you start with the big picture and progress to the small bits, you'll find that it's as they say: "By the inch it's a cinch, but by the mile, it's a pile." If you work from the last to the first and break it all down into small bits, anything can be accomplished.

Whether I'm writing a book, giving a seminar, traveling somewhere, or putting on a tour for a group, I follow this principle. For instance, I planned a tour to Greece with my students, where we'd be studying the philosophy of the Greeks in their own land and environment. I dreamed it down to the last detail. Then I worked my way back until I knew exactly what action steps to take each day to make the trip a possibility.

If you apply this idea to your plans and goals, anything is possible. Follow the Law of Finale to your dreams—and to your amazing life.

WORDS OF POWER

*My dreams are now possible, for I take small steps
toward them every day.*

*I start with the final dream in mind and work my
way back to its accomplishment.*

I see my goals and then find the details.

*I keep the final outcome before me,
and I break it down to daily action steps.*

I live the life I love as I do the daily action steps leading to my dreams.

I manifest the life I love, for I know the last is first and the first is last.

MY WORDS OF POWER

MY REFLECTIONS

How can I use the Law of Finale today to fulfill my life's
purpose, dreams, and objectives?

_____

_____

_____

_____

_____

_____

_____

_____

✦✦✦✦✦

Conclusion

Since you've just finished reading *You Can Have an Amazing Life . . . in Just 60 Days*, it's now wise to reflect for a while on all the laws you've read. If you've just read the book for the first time, take a day to digest the broad principles before diving in for your second, more focused, reading. (If you've just read the book for the second time and have spent 60 days with these laws, again pause, consider, and make notes to yourself.)

Then, as soon as you can, begin to read this book once again, either one law per day or once again straight through. You can't put your heart and mind into these magical pages without some of their amazing ideas sticking with you. You can't read the Words of Power without their essence staying with you, and you can't write your own Words of Power without transforming your life. By reflecting on the laws once again, each will become ever more realized in your daily life.

The second time you review this book, you'll experience yet another shift, a greater transformation, and you'll become even more awakened to a brand-new you. You've embarked on an ongoing journey that will continue for the rest of your life, so stay with this daily action and watch what happens to you over time. Don't be surprised when others tell you, "Wow, you truly have an amazing life!" By living these 60 laws on a daily basis, abundant wealth in all areas of your life—spiritual, mental, professional, financial, familial, social, and physical—can be yours.

Love your amazing life!

✦✦✦✦✦

Acknowledgments

Seldom, if ever, is a book a product of one individual's effort, and this is certainly true of what you've just read. So I give openhearted thanks to my transcriptionist, Anna Plant, for her diligent work in transforming my recorded words into an initial written text and more legible draft; my editor, Karen Risch, for her work and expertise in transforming my partly unclear verbiage into readable and understandable language; my final editors Jill Kramer and Shannon Littrell of Hay House for adding the final touches and polishing this jewel; and my publisher, Hay House, for making it possible for this book to be read by a great number of people. I also acknowledge all the individuals from whom I've learned, and who've provided me living stories from which these amazing laws have been derived.

About the Author

Dr. John F. Demartini is an international speaker and consultant who breathes life and enthusiasm into his audiences with his enlightening perspectives, humorous observations of human nature, and practical action steps. When he speaks, hearts open, minds become inspired, and people are moved to action. His gentle, fun, and informative teachings mingle entertaining stories with transformational wisdom and insights. His trailblazing philosophy and revolutionary understanding is reshaping modern psychology and business and transforming the lives of millions. As a researcher, writer, philosopher, and retired chiropractor, his studies have made him a leading expert on healing, human potential, and philosophy.

Dr. Demartini lives on a ship that travels to the most beautiful ports throughout the world. In these elite and exotic settings, he's often chauffeured in a white-and-gold Rolls Royce . . . to speak to, inspire, and serve millions of people globally. A regular on television and radio talk shows, he's also a prolific writer and enjoys hanging out with some of the movers and shakers of the world. A millionaire with homes in several locations internationally, Dr. Demartini lives the life of his dreams with those he loves. It's truly an amazing life!

Notes

Notes

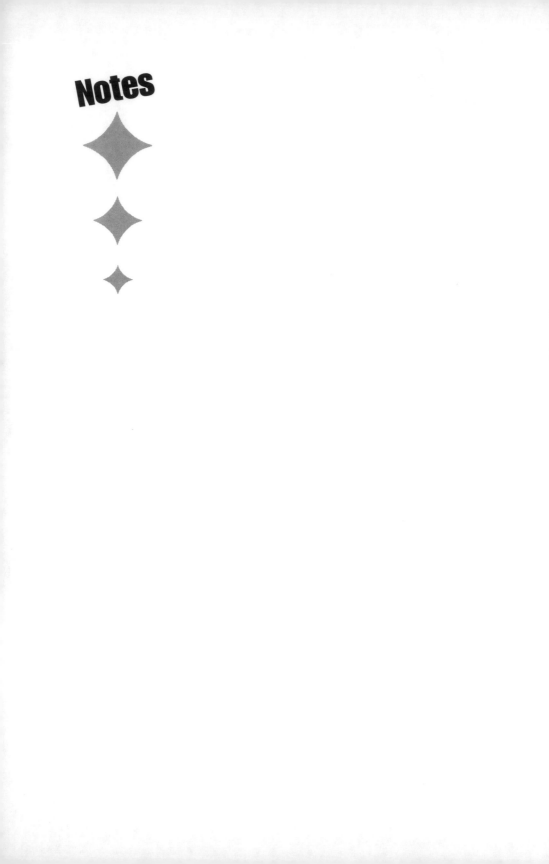

Notes

Notes

Notes

Notes

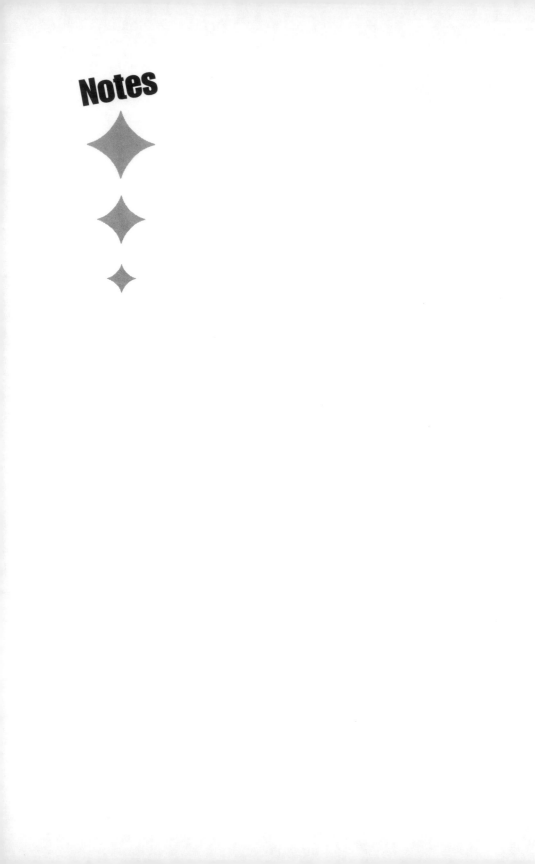

Notes

Notes

Notes

We hope you enjoyed this Hay House book. If you'd like to receive a free catalog featuring additional Hay House books and products, or if you'd like information about the Hay Foundation, please contact:

Hay House, Inc.
P.O. Box 5100
Carlsbad, CA 92018-5100

(760) 431-7695 or **(800) 654-5126**
(760) 431-6948 (fax) or **(800) 650-5115 (fax)**
www.hayhouse.com®

Published and distributed in Australia by:
Hay House Australia Pty. Ltd., 18/36 Ralph St., Alexandria NSW 2015
Phone: 612-9669-4299 • *Fax:* 612-9669-4144 • www.hayhouse.com.au

Published and distributed in the United Kingdom by:
Hay House UK, Ltd., 292B Kensal Rd., London W10 5BE • *Phone:* 44-20-8962-1230
Fax: 44-20-8962-1239 • www.hayhouse.co.uk

Published and distributed in the Republic of South Africa by:
Hay House SA (Pty), Ltd., P.O. Box 990, Witkoppen 2068
Phone/Fax: 27-11-706-6612 • orders@psdprom.co.za

Published in India by:
Hay House Publishers India, Muskaan Complex, Plot No. 3, B-2, Vasant Kunj,
New Delhi 110 070 • *Phone:* 91-11-4176-1620 • *Fax:* 91-11-4176-1630
www.hayhouseindia.co.in

Distributed in Canada by: Raincoast,
9050 Shaughnessy St., Vancouver, B.C. V6P 6E5
Phone: (604) 323-7100 • *Fax:* (604) 323-2600 • www.raincoast.com

Tune in to **HayHouseRadio.com**® for the best in inspirational talk radio featuring top Hay House authors! And, sign up via the Hay House USA Website to receive the Hay House online newsletter and stay informed about what's going on with your favorite authors. You'll receive bimonthly announcements about Discounts and Offers, Special Events, Product Highlights, Free Excerpts, Giveaways, and more!
www.hayhouse.com®